REAL MAN ADVENTURES

REAL MAN
ADVENTURES

T COOPER

M<small>c</small>SWEENEY'S BOOKS
SAN FRANCISCO

McSWEENEY'S BOOKS
SAN FRANCISCO

www.mcsweeneys.net

McSweeney's and colophon are registered trademarks of McSweeney's,
a privately held company with wildly fluctuating resources.

ISBN: 978-1-938073-00-7

For whom else but my wife

CONTENTS

VISIBLE

It goes a long way back, some twenty years. All my life I had been looking for something, and everywhere I turned someone tried to tell me what it was. I accepted their answers too, though they were often in contradiction and even self-contradictory. —Ralph Ellison, *Invisible Man*[1]

I AM A VISIBLE MAN. By all appearances white, middle-class, heterosexual. Male.

Blessed, right? What everybody wants to be, when it comes down to it. I earn 25 percent more than women, for some unexplained

---

1. p. 43: Second Vintage International Edition (Random House Inc.), 1995

reason statisticians have never seemed to be able to make sense of on paper. I don't get beaten and sexually assaulted, traded and married off, shrouded in black fabric or have my genitals mutilated, and I am not readily found removing my clothes for members of the opposite sex in ubiquitous venues open all hours of the day. (Okay, Chippendales, but no lady actually has fun at Chippendales or ever returns even if she has a little fun in Vegas once.) I am the perennial buyer, never the seller. And if she's not selling, I can usually just take, one way or another. History tells me so.

If you woke up one day—or no, say you're an embryo before it figures out whether it's going to have a Y chromosome or not, and you can decide what you are going to be; you could go to the public library, take all the dusty books off the shelf and really get a good look at all of time and see who's generally come out on top—what would you be?

If you were a betting zygote, and you wanted to survive, and more than survive you wanted to have, like, an in-ground pool and attached garage and maybe a little cushion of land between you and the next guy, and not get raped over and over and generally be left to do what you wish, there's only one clear choice. You'd grab that Y chromosome. And if you couldn't annex the actual chromosome, you'd probably find some other way to go about it.

That's what I did!

I did it for the extra 25 percent. And the power. And the respect I command in merely walking down the sidewalk, or stating my wishes plainly.

Except that's not entirely the case.

It turns out if you scratch off a layer I become slightly less visible: a Jew. Slough off another, and I disappear a bit more: not so white. A large percent of people I come across actually take me for Puerto Rican, Arab, somehow brown ("swarthy," my mother-in-law pronounced me when my then-future wife showed her a photo). If I'm in dirty dungarees and working in the yard or on the house, neighbors jogging by or walking their dogs assume I'm a day laborer. Strangers will often speak Spanish to me if not leading with "Do you speak English?" when in need of directions on the street. Or sometimes folks will address me as "my friend" (as in, Hey, my friend. I'm going to ask you this question which you look like you couldn't possibly know the answer to, except I'm really desperate and you're the only person here, so I might as well give it a shot and cross my fingers I'm not insulting you), which is when you really know white people believe they are talking to a nonwhite person. And nowadays I get "randomly" selected for additional screening at the airport sometimes, since I also apparently give terrorist realness.

Finally, go for that last layer, the one I put there myself without anybody's (or nature's) help. Yank it off quick before I notice. It hurts like shit but if you do it fast like I said, the pain doesn't last long. And then I pretty much disappear altogether. A traitor, a spy.

> At the landing I saw a bucket full of kerosene and seized it, flinging it impulsively into a burning room. A huge puff of smoke-fringed flame filled the doorway, licking outward toward me. I ran, choking and coughing as I plunged. They did it themselves, I thought, holding my breath—planned it, organized it, applied the flame.[2]

---

2. Ibid, p. 549.

What I just did there was quickly fan through the pages of *Invisible Man* and randomly stick a finger down, and then typed in the paragraph my finger landed on. As random as whether a sperm cell carries an X or Y chromosome into the egg it's fertilizing. Or is it? Because from where I sit right now, about to blast all this shit of mine into a world that's already on fire and then spill accelerant all over it… it feels like either the smartest[3] or stupidest[4] thing I've ever done. I don't believe there's an in-between.

---

3. Outside of asking my wife to marry me.

4. Outside of trying for three years in college to have a floppy Hugh Grant haircut with nothing but a Jew-fro to work with.

WWDD?

AFTER I READ HIS memoir, *Half a Life*, I mentioned to the author Darin Strauss that I was thinking about writing about my "thing," the way he wrote about his "thing"—the one thing that defines most of us (whether determined by others or ourselves). He wrote me this:

> As for what you write next: if you don't want to write that, don't. It seems wildly personal, and so if you feel uncomfortable, listen to that. This book took twenty-eight years for me to even START. But thanks for being so nice about it.

So What Would Darin Do? He managed to wrestle his thing out of him—and quite beautifully at that. But he also said I could wait on my thing. Or not do it at all. Somewhere therein lay perhaps just the permission I needed to type that Ellison passage, and begin to find out whether I even could.

I don't really want to write about this thing of mine, but I think I might have to—to stop it from being a thing. If that's possible. I could certainly regret it later, like I've regretted candor on a few distinct occasions in the past.[1] It's just that nowadays, one's candor and the resultant exposure can end up hanging around forever for people to pick through. My kids, for example, who in a couple years can and probably will get on the Internet to read all they can about the subject. Just one Google search and something my wife and I have taken great pains and sensitivity and a bunch of time and effort to explain and share with them in the safe, accepting, and loving environment of our household can be unraveled in an instant. Because when one's candor is filtered through another human being, especially one with a little more power, the results can be devastating (see: all of history). So I suppose this book is an attempt to be my own filter, leaving me nobody to blame but myself when it all goes pear-shaped.

Well, me and Darin Strauss. A difference being that his "secret" (at eighteen having been involved in an auto vs. bicycle accident that left a female schoolmate dead) was something he could (and did successfully) hide for many years after leaving home. I cannot reliably hide that I was not always the man I am today.

Certainly, when I meet people for the first time, none know my "secret" (or more accurately, my past, which many confuse with a secret). But there will always be people whose history has paralleled

---

1. See the chapter in this book entitled "The Little Surfer Girl," for example.

and intersected my own—from family to colleagues to that girl
Annika in the second grade who ate powdered soap at recess—and
without a complete name and identity change accompanied by
renouncing my entire history (something I'm unwilling to do, as
tempting as it sometimes seems), it is near impossible for me to live
completely stealthily as a man in this world, because, simply, I was
not born male. Not in any conventional sense, at least. Not according to science.

I HOPE YOU'RE SITTING DOWN

*Letter to My Parents I Contemplated Publishing in a
Men's Magazine to Let Them (My Parents) Know
I Wasn't Their Daughter Anymore*

[EARLY 2009]

Dear Mom and Dad,

I know this is going to be a complete shock to you, not to mention a huge disappointment, but there's something I have to tell you, and I hope you're sitting down.

I'm not gay.

There, I said it. It's out there, and I can't take it back.

But before you start freaking out, I want to give you the good news. Not only am I not gay, but I'm so not gay that I'm engaged to be married, plus am now stepdad to my fiancée's two beautiful blonde children. We all live in a nice four-bedroom, two-and-a-half bath house and have two hybrid cars, two rescue pit bulls, and a gray-and-white cat that I don't like very much.

It's everything you've ever wanted for me! I do yard work. And carpool. I'm completely normal, as in, there's nothing you have to be embarrassed about with friends and family anymore—no more peroxided buzz cuts, no faux-hawks or combat boots, no bringing home anarcho-vegan dates with septum piercings. No more homo anything at all! So you can just send those PFLAG brochures back to be recycled for somebody who actually needs them.

But there's also some bad news, and I suppose I should share that with you, too. I know it's not really cool that you're finding all this out about me in the pages of a magazine, but to be completely honest, for years I've been worried you'd reject me for not being gay, and terrified that you might decide to cut me out of your life completely. But you raised me to tell the truth to both myself and others, so in that spirit I feel as though I need to "come out" to you even more explicitly:

I am a heterosexual man.

Let me take you back. Remember how good I was at football? Like, really good? How I was riding motorcycles at an age when most kids were learning to bicycle without training wheels? And how you had to promise me several pairs of shorts and pants in exchange for buying one gauzy dress to wear to Spencer Presler's bar mitzvah? Or flash forward a little, to 2002. Mom, remember when you came to one of my readings for my first book, and there was a big poster with my picture on it, and it repeatedly referred to me as "he"? You seemed very alarmed and notified the bookseller of the "mistake," but you never mentioned it again. Or Dad, that time years before that when we were out at a restaurant in Santa Fe, and you thought I was the maître d' and asked, "Sir, when will our table be ready?" I just said, "Dad, it's me," and you chirped, "Oh," and then we sat down and enjoyed our Tex-Mex dinner.

Or let's get even more contemporary. As an author, I'm fortunate to have my work mentioned or appear in various media, and you might've noticed that nowadays that media refers to me as "he." For a couple of years, there was no gender pronoun, and other times, like in the *New York Times Book Review*, a writer will go out of her way to make sure that her audience knows I am a "she" (the reviewer was wrong, but whatever[1]). Either way, I know you've seen a lot of this stuff, because you've always been supportive of me and my work and you enjoy sharing in it. But I guess what I'm getting at is whether this news is even really a surprise to you at all.

I'm not quite one of those "born in the wrong body" types you see on *Oprah* or The Learning Channel. I actually think I was born in the right body, my body. It's just a little different, and doesn't fit squarely into the gender binary. But I think you've suspected that

---

1. Actually, not whatever. That was fucked up, and it has eaten at me for years. I have considered writing the *Times* to ask for a correction, but what's the use? How would I explain to them that in their reviews of "normal" people, reviewers don't take the time out to straighten out readers' assumptions about an author's identity: "By the way, Jonathan Franzen is a heterosexual white male." There was no gender pronoun on my book at the time; there was certainly no female gender pronoun on any of my own press materials or Web site. It was a violation for the reviewer to state unequivocally in a paper of record that I am female. It was simply not true. Not then, maybe not ever.

I keep hoping one day I'll stop caring, but short of a complete correction in that goddam review that will likely be around for the rest of time (plus a gilded letter of apology and fruit basket from the reviewer), I don't know if that particular parenthetical will ever stop bunching my boxers.

all along. You of all people, in fact, have known about the kind of kid I was, and the kind of person I've grown up to be: mostly well-intentioned and seeking to do right by others, moderately creative, often stubborn, but generally pleasant to be around. I haven't been tortured or miserable or beaten senseless on the playground because of my life experience—in fact, quite the opposite. Sometimes it even seemed like I fit in a little too well, made it look a little too easy. Not that it's always been a cakewalk (there was the time on the subway at knifepoint), but for the most part I've been quite lucky.

In truth, the most pain I've had over being a straight guy comes from my fears about how you would react. I can't front and say I haven't daydreamed about your passing before I'd have to explain all of this to you (because it would of course kill you anyway). So you can see why coming home for the holidays might be a little tricky this year. There's my beard, for starters. Then there's the fact that my children know me as their stepfather, and they won't know who you're talking about when you continuously call me your "daughter," rapid-fire repeating it to anyone and everyone as though the more it's said, the more it might go back to being true.

You no longer have a daughter. But you do have granddaughters. And they really want to meet the people responsible for making me into the kind of person who figured out that he wasn't what others decided he was, evolving instead into something else entirely.

Love,
Me

NOT THE MAN THEY THINK I AM AT HOME

Excerpts from a Draft of the Letter I Eventually Sent My Parents to Let Them Know That I Wasn't Their Daughter Anymore

...THE GOOD NEWS IS: I don't think it's a giant mystery to you that I don't identify as female. Sexual identity and gender identity are two entirely different (though of course not completely unrelated) things; one is who you're attracted to, the other is who you are. I know for years you've just assumed I was gay—because of who I've been romantically involved with. But it's not as simple as that—in fact, I don't think I ever actually "came out" to you as anything, sexual-identity speaking. I was just me, and this was who I was dating at any particular time. In truth, I never really felt gay at all, and that's why those words never came out of my mouth. Not once. And the word *lesbian*? I have never and would never use that term in reference to myself. Never. In fact, I'm probably one of the most lesbophobic people on the planet, probably because of my own fucked-up issues of not wanting to be assumed to be one. I got no beef with lesbians; I'm just not one. I've never seen even one episode of *The L-Word*. Never been to the Michigan Womyn's Festival, don't know who Dinah Shore is, and certainly never donned a thumb ring or ear cuff....

...As far as my gender goes, I know it's been obvious to you for years that my gender presentation is not normative, that is, it has never really fit perfectly into the male/female binary. It's always fallen somewhere in between, and in the past decade or so, it has organically migrated to the male side of the spectrum. I don't know how else to say it, but: I'm basically a dude....

...I love you and always will. This has nothing to do with you, anything you did or didn't do. (It's not because you didn't breast-feed me, Ma.) I'm the same person I've always been, regardless of gender or whom I sleep with, have relationships with, what my haircut looks like, books I write, what I wear, where I live, whom I socialize with, how frequently I go to the gym—any of these and several other things you've agonized over in the past. I am not "a man trapped in a woman's body." That's asinine. I was born in the body I was born into; I'm not trapped, but I am a man. I know you've heard me say stuff like this in the past, both publicly and privately; I know you've seen some of this material pop up in some of my writing, at readings in the form of questions from the audience about my characters, or in interviews. I know you have been with me when people refer to me as "he," and you have flustered many a waitperson when referring to me as "she" or "your daughter" when there is nothing but what looks like a son sitting at the table next to you....

...If you can, please try to hear me, and not whatever you might've seen or heard on this topic; it's not like the pregnant man on *Oprah*, or the lady on *Maury* who didn't know she'd married a guy who had not been born male. It's not like what you've read in your PFLAG pamphlets or online about "roid rage." I don't turn into the Incredible Hulk at intervals (if only). I have not been tortured and miserable for years and years suppressing some deep, dark secret that I've been afraid would come out and destroy me and my family; my experience is completely my own. It's not a "hard life," certainly not harder than most others' on this planet. I know this may be forever impossible for you to understand, but this is nothing for you to worry about: it's simply, for me, the most natural thing in the world.

KICK ME

"KICK ME" IS A game I used to play with my brother (seven years my senior).

Object: to land a kick anywhere on your opponent's body (including crotch, face, etc.).

Rules: none.

Play: Kickee repeats, "Kick me, kick me, kick me," over and over, enticing and taunting kicker. Kicker becomes kickee as soon as a kick is landed, play swapping back and forth.

Game ends: In tears (on part of younger sibling), or when mother has screamed, "STOP IT!"

My brother always initiated, placing a hand on my forehead to keep me at arm's length, and then repeating, "Kick me" however many times were required before I could resist no more, and with all my strength and determination would try to kick him, usually in one of the shins. I cannot recall an occasion on which I was actually able to land a solid kick. Thus, the only time I would be allowed to be the kickee would be when my brother tricked me into a game by "letting" me go first.

His being appreciably older, significantly stronger, bigger, and not a little meaner, I stood small chance of being a formidable opponent. My arms were of course not long enough, nor was I tall enough to palm his forehead and keep him away in that manner, so my method of staying outside the range of his half-hearted kicks would involve darting back and forth like Barry Sanders (I fancied), bobbing and weaving, hiding under things, throwing people in front of me to block my brother's foot, whatever it took to stay alive and stave off becoming the kicker for as long as possible. But inevitably he would catch me, and even though he'd pull his kicks, it would still hurt like shit when one would land. But I'd hold it together, take my turn, and like Charlie Brown and that goddam football, I'd fool myself: this time I'll connect.

I don't have a lot of extremely vivid memories of my childhood, but I do have a distinct one of a particular game of Kick Me. It was the first big family trip my parents saved up for and took us on, to Europe, when I was about six, my brother thirteen or fourteen. I loved traveling, thrilled at seeing novel places and people and things, but my brother, not so much: he was a zitty, pissy pubert with little power in the world but to torture me. My mother claims her most persistent memories of that trip involve her two children traversing the Champs Elysées, Saint Mark's Square, and Westminster Abbey, with him tormenting, "Kick me, kick me, kick me." Him walking backwards, teasing, taunting, laughing at my repeated failure, and me trailing with a face damp and red, pigeons scattering.

We were somewhere in the French countryside, alongside the Seine, when I took a giant swing at him and missed, losing my balance and quickly finding myself on my ass, my hands ground into the gravel on the curb beneath me. We must've been on a small traffic island, because I looked up and there were cars whizzing by on either side. My mother grabbed my upper arm and dragged me to my feet across the street, where I finally got a look at the pebbles deeply embedded in both palms, purple with blood just starting to ooze out.

I will always remember the magic—no other word for it—of seeing the Eiffel Tower for the first time, and Notre Dame, Buckingham Palace, the *Mona Lisa*. Of floating on a Venice canal. But I will also likely never forget the dysphoria of rage, feeling so tiny and insignificant. Both in the realm of my family and in the larger world I was seeing for the first time. Inconsequential, weak. So easily taken, forced into a position. Despising my brother's ability to play me, to enrage to the point of tears. Hating him so much, when maybe I just wanted to see what it would be like to be him.

SOMETIMES I THINK THE WHOLE OF MODERN HISTORY CAN BE EXPLAINED BY TESTOSTERONE

IN MY "JOURNEY," THERE have been some new truths, even if they are also stereotypes:

1. I don't cry as much as I used to. Or: It takes way more to make me cry.
2. I am angry more frequently. Or: It takes way less to make me blazing mad.
3. I don't get as bummed out by things as I used to. Or: my mood is generally positive.
4. I have less patience.
5. I am not as adept at communicating.
6. I want to have relations with my wife, all of the time, regardless of context.

7. People defer to me more.[1]
8. I am stronger, my muscle mass larger.
9. I have more stamina on the treadmill.
10. I say less to strangers.

---

1. This may seem far-fetched and like I'm trying to seem like a good feminist or some bullshit, but ask my wife: she'll gladly confirm it happens all the time when we are out in public or meeting new people. (And she is no shrinking violet.)

A BRIEF INTERVIEW I DID FOR *ESQUIRE*'S "HOW TO BE A MAN" ISSUE, FROM WHICH MY ANSWERS WERE EXCLUDED IN FAVOR OF INSIGHTS FROM GUYS LIKE TOM CRUISE

ESQUIRE: WHAT'S THE GREATEST example you know, or have witnessed, of someone stepping up as man?

TC: The first example that comes to mind is pretty much anything Johnny Weir does. Outside of that, honesty always leaves a big impression. Across the board, across gender, the bravery required to be completely honest with both oneself and others is something that is as rare as it is great. So to me "stepping up and being a man" is twofold: it means trying to be as honorable as possible, and in cases where you fail to be as honorable as possible, then it is to be completely honest about that shortcoming—without being mean or punitive. It's more about being an adult than being a man.

ESQ: What about manhood do you know now that you wish you'd known at eighteen?

TC: 1) That men aren't right all the time, or even most of the time. 2) That men don't have to act like they're right when they know they're wrong. 3) That you can still be a man, even if you don't have a manhood.[1]

ESQ: What's your favorite thing about being a man?

TC: Just "being a man" is something I can't take for granted, since I was not born a man. But you know what? It turns out nobody else is born a man either. Sure, roughly half of us humans are born male—but only a fraction of that fraction grow into men.

So I'd have to say my number-one favorite thing about being a man is being a man. Because it wasn't something that just happened to me. I had to work for it—going against what the world was telling me I was ever since I was pushed out of my mother and into it.

Other favorite things about being a man include (in no particular order): sideburns, sex drive, not feeling paralyzed with worry about everyone else's feelings all the time, and the unconditional acceptance from and love of the best woman in the world, which has probably made me more of a man than any of the other shit out there—including testosterone.

---

1. While I know these three things in theory, that doesn't mean I am very good at them or necessarily remember them all of the time in practice.

THE CLOSEST I'VE EVER COME TO WRITING A POEM, NOT COUNTING WHEN YOU ARE FORCED TO DO SO IN GRADE SCHOOL

FEAR[1]

She has me stripped and flayed and is swinging at will from the inside of my rib cage as if on one of those geodesic playground apparatuses. Primary paint colors and rust flakes in her hands, she's free-climbing all limbs and laughs and smiles, and we are both eight and eighty years young, and we are also unicorns riding clouds and cotton candy kittens, and every puppy who ever fell in love with a wiry tomboy's skinned knees. And the air is perfect up here, even if the walls are rattling and cells are dividing and then (somewhat hauntingly) regenerating, only with her DNA in them.

---

1. Written about a few months after meeting my wife.

And sometimes—in fact most times if I'm honest—when she leaves whatever room I'm in, I am instantaneously seized with the distinct notion that she might never come back. Not ever. And not quite seized, rather more like doubled over in the driver's seat in long-term parking row 14A, the minutes just about to click over into another day's rate, mouth carved into a grotesque howl, the sort where no sound comes out but the hiss of compressed air. And to be further honest, it's not only when she leaves the room, but generally anytime her eyes leave mine (to drive, to walk, to read, to see something else).

There it is, the signpost up ahead: not the man she and the world need you to be.

WHY THEY'RE CALLED *PASS*PORTS

PARTIAL TRANSCRIPT OF A telephone conversation I had with a representative of the U.S. Department of State[1] [after having my passport renewal application rejected and returned in the mail]:

ME: I don't understand what the problem is. You have my fee, you have my correctly filled-out application, and you have a letter from a surgeon saying that I had sexual reassignment surgery and have lived as a man for several years.

DEPARTMENT OF STATE: It doesn't say you had complete sexual reassignment surgery.

---

1. This was shortly after Barack Obama became president and Hillary Clinton secretary of state.

ME: I see. Well, what does complete sexual reassignment surgery entail?

DOS: Um. [*Ruffles papers*]. It requires, um. It requires full, complete surgery.

ME: What is full, complete surgery?

DOS: What you are calling "bottom" surgery.

ME: So essentially, in order to have a passport that I can safely travel with, I need to disclose what is in my pants.

DOS: I suppose you could put it that way.

ME: So I could have a penis and giant boobs but you'd still let me have the M?

DOS: I didn't make up the rule, sir; I'm just telling you what it says.

ME: Did you have to tell the government what is in your pants in order to get your passport?

DOS: Uh, sir, I did not have to, no.

ME: Does it seem fair that I have to?

DOS: I can't speak to that.

ME: You—

DOS: I'm sorry. I just need evidence of complete sexual reassignment surgery, and then I can process your application.

ME: The doctor says he considers it full sexual reassignment surgery.

DOS: It needs to say complete.

ME: Okay, so you're telling me I need to go to Zagreb, Croatia, and spend like fifty thousand dollars on a far-from-perfect procedure that would give me essentially a limp piece of sirloin hanging between my legs for you to issue me a passport with an M on it?

DOS: Again, I didn't make up the policy. I just need something that says you've had complete sexual reassignment surgery.

ME: I have completed my transition.

DOS: Not according to the guidelines.

ME: Whose guidelines?

DOS: The Department of State's.

ME: What about my guidelines? What if I'm okay with how I am? Actually, why don't you just tell me how many inches of penis the government requires to decide I'm male?

DOS: [*Agitated*] I don't know.

ME: No, seriously. How long? Because maybe I'll just make it under the wire.

DOS: I don't know.

ME: Okay, then. What if I don't have either? Like, what if you can't tell? What do those people get?

DOS: —

ME: Or… [*raised voice*] what if I don't want to discuss with a complete stranger and put down on record with the government what I have down there, because it's nobody's business except mine and whomever I share it with?[2]

---

2. On that note, what the hell is up with the Transportation Safety Administration's new full-body scanners at airports? The ones that reveal intimate contours of travelers' bodies, i.e., take three-dimensional images of your completely NUDE body underneath your clothing, aka strip search you without probable cause, aka violate the Fourth Amendment and the Privacy Act (images are sometimes stored, and they reveal things like prosthetic breasts or testicles, colostomy bags, catheters, and other potentially embarrassing—not to mention private—details on all kinds of people's bodies).

So essentially, any time I travel through an airport where one of the new scanners is in use, if I suck it up and go through the machine (instead of drawing extra attention to myself by requesting an invasive, time-consuming pat-down

DOS: —

ME: [*Calmer*] This is just intensely personal, and I'm uncomfortable having to talk about this with you just to be able to travel freely and comfortably in the world.

DOS: I can assure you it's not entirely comfortable for me either.

ME: I know you're trying to help. Can I ask you one more thing?

DOS: [*Sighing*] Yes.

ME: All those guys in Iraq getting their genitals blown off by IEDs, do you make them change their passports from M to F when they come home, because they don't have penises anymore?

DOS: I don't know what you want me to say. Send me a letter that says you've had complete gender reassignment surgery, and I'll process your application.

…Which I took as tacit permission to forge a document with the required wording. Two weeks later in the mail was my new passport with the correct gender marker on it.

Less than a year after that, once President Obama's appointees

---

instead), I am outed. And ashamed. And standing there on the yellow footprints for a couple minutes just hoping I don't get harassed—or worse—when stopping by the restroom prior to boarding my flight.

had some time to review the old policy on issuing passports to transgender citizens, the State Department's rules were loosened. Now all you need to get your gender changed is to present a letter from a physician stating that you have undergone clinical treatment for "gender transition." Which is appropriately, graciously vague,

and means you can be on hormones, not be on hormones, be on a low dose of hormones or a full dose of hormones, have had surgery, have not had surgery, have had one kind of surgery but not others, and so on.

I had a feeling the guy I talked to at the State Department knew that the new rules were coming. (Transgender legal advocacy organizations had been working to educate past administrations for years; this was the first one willing to budge.) Or maybe I was just telling myself he knew that as I repeatedly practiced forging a signature and Photoshopping letterhead—and tried desperately not to think about the fact that I was defrauding the government and would of course ultimately be caught and end up in federal prison for several years for my brazen counterfeiting scheme.

But how would they determine which prison to throw me in?

DREAM SEQUENCE

I FEEL PRETTY STRONGLY that whenever writers write about their dreams in essays or memoirs, the dreams are vastly fictionalized. For obvious reasons. That said, and with full recognition that every story is altered to some extent by the retelling, I am going to attempt to recount faithfully a dream I had two nights ago:

I was being harassed by a few policemen on a random street. When asked, I showed them my driver's license. While I was still pretty certain the policemen were going to let me go, I remember feeling relief that my paperwork was in order. I believe, but I cannot completely recall, that I was also asked to produce my passport, in addition to other random paperwork.

At some point I was suddenly arrested and taken into custody. I don't know the cause, but it made some sort of sense to me as I was being loaded into an unmarked van with a bunch of other people (both males and females, all of us cuffed with hands resting in our laps) and driven to a prison that looked like a cross between San Quentin and every Midwestern prison you see on MSNBC's *Lockup*. Outside the facility, we were joined by a few other vans full of prisoners, and as we exited the vehicles, we were all funneled into one line leading downhill toward the prison. After a dozen or so yards, a group of guards separated us into two lines—male and female— that fed into two different, side-by-side doors to the facility. I was put into the male line. I remember thinking all of it felt suspiciously like Buchenwald, but there was nobody to whom I might whisper the observation, as was my impulse.

The lines moved very slowly, and for a time, the general atmosphere and my state of mind were calm. I didn't question where I was, or fight it. I felt like I just needed to suck it up, serve my time, and then I would be free and all this would be behind me. It wasn't like I was certain a mistake had been made, there had been grave injustice, or that I wasn't supposed to be there (as usually is the case in my persecution dreams). As I inched ahead in line, though, and caught a glimpse of what was happening up ahead, I started to panic (only on the inside). There was a female guard with a rifle near me, standing between the two lines of prisoners, and I tried to get her attention. I was definitely the shortest and slightest guy in line. Nobody had paid me any particular mind before, but as soon as I started entreating the guard, a few people from both lines started to take notice, the way people get when somebody cuts in front of them at the movie concession stand or at Kmart. I coughed a few times until the female guard looked in my direction, at which point I tried to make my face really kind and open, to entice her to come over. She appeared at first impassive, but then it seemed as if she might be wavering. I assumed she would ultimately decide to ignore me, but just as I was getting to the front of the line and a male guard asked me to pull down my pants (revealing just the hair on my stomach and the beginning of the trail below that), the female guard finally came over and leaned in close to my lips. I think she had seen how panicked the look on my face was as I reluctantly started to pull my pants down.

At this point the dream became more like a scene in a film, where I was observing from a different perspective than that of myself in line. Now I was one character among a cast of many. What I saw was a small, dark-haired dude (me) talking to a guard, but at the same time I could also see people in both the men's and women's lines noticing that I was talking to this female guard, perhaps trying to curry special treatment. It was like I could understand it from their perspectives, too. I don't know precisely what was said to the guard because of that perspective—even though I was the one saying it. I did have a sense of what must have been conveyed to her, which was that I couldn't pull my pants all the way down for the strip search, because then both the other men and some women would see me and know that I was different. That if that happened, I would of course be beaten and raped when we got into the general population on the other side of the male and female admitting areas.

The guard immediately understood. Not in a nurturing, kind way, but rather in the way that suggested she and the other guards must've had a memo or perhaps a sensitivity training session about "these kind of people who you might see in the prison population," and she was just following protocol to keep me out of danger. Doing her job.

So while a few of the other prisoners looked on, again, from both lines, I was back in myself (no longer a player in the scene I was watching), and the guard led me into a separate chamber to take off all my clothes and put on an orange prison uniform while she and a few other male guards looked the other way. I was given my requisite supplies and the number of my cell. And then I was released back into the general population, among other men and women carrying their blankets and towels and soap toward their cells. I walked by rows and rows of open cells, which were divided by gender, two or four people per cell. There was the stainless-steel toilet in the middle of each room, completely on view for all to see. I was immediately terrified by the prospect of having to sit down to pee in front of everybody, but then I remembered that the female guard had acted like everything was okay, so I told myself it would indeed be okay, just keep walking and try to find the right cell. Two women inmates in orange jumpsuits approached me then, as I neared the common part of the prison (gym equipment, Ping-Pong table, TV). They spoke to me sympathetically, like they knew my "secret," and would help me keep it from the men in the joint.

One of the women looked at my paper and pointed to a small cell that was more like a compartment that you see in Japanese airports or business commuter hotels. I had to climb the wall to enter the tiny space, but it would be all my own, no cellmates. Just a bedroll and the small adjacent cement surface to put things on. A notebook and pen and alarm clock were all I really had, besides linens. As I was slowly setting these few things up in my space, the sympathetic women whispered something about how another person with "concerns like mine" had just been there the month before—and they pointed out the private small bathroom that he'd had access to for showering and toilets. I remember feeling immense relief at this idea, but then also equal amounts of fear that guys would see me going in and out of the bathroom enough times that one or two of them would eventually figure it out, and the information about something being different about me would spread from there. I asked one of the girls how we were supposed to know how long we were to be confined, but they said it varied.

At dinner and free time before bed, everything seemed normal. When it was lights-out and the barred door slammed me shut inside my pod, I remember feeling completely safe, but as I lay there listening to the night sounds of the prison with the ceiling alarmingly close to my nose, I was thinking to myself over and over: *that door is going to fly open first thing in the morning.* Thinking, *I'm going to have to act tough and like nothing's out of the ordinary. Fake irritable bowel syndrome, or colitis.* I was thinking, *At least I have as many tattoos as a lot of these guys, even if I can't bench press a lot,* and I lay there sleeplessly trying to figure the complicated algebra in my head: how many guys would see me use the bathroom and showers how many times per day, how exponentially fast that information would travel, and then how many weeks that would buy me before the worst would happen. Which I knew would happen; it was only a matter of how long I could last.

THE LITTLE SURFER GIRL

NOT TOO LONG AGO I was interviewed in person by a reporter for the *LA Weekly*, the main alternative paper in my native Los Angeles. The story was to appear in a front-of-the-book column, just six or seven hundred words (of the style—if not the quality—of the *New Yorker's* "The Talk of the Town" department). My book[1] at that time had just appeared on the *Los Angeles Times* bestseller list for a couple weeks, and I had been in town for events at local bookstores a few weeks prior to that.

When the reporter showed up at my folks' house (where I was staying), she seemed nice enough. It was my last day in town, and

---

1. A graphic novel about a polar bear who attempts to escape extinction by going to Hollywood. There is nothing in the book explicitly transgender at all.

I didn't necessarily want to spend that time doing an interview. But I did, for three hours. I don't need to go into all of the details, but suffice to say that I made an amiable connection with the reporter, she seemed sympathetic and easygoing, and she laughed at my jokes pretty consistently throughout the interview. She also seemed to enjoy herself, as was confirmed by a follow-up e-mail she sent me: "It was great talking with you. A lot of people I interview get caught up in their own hype. But you say what's on your mind. It's refreshing."

About a quarter of the way through the interview, the reporter mentioned that she was surprised to learn from my publisher's publicist that I had not been born male. She then asked me, "When did you have the surgery?" at which point I calmly, non-defensively, launched into the requisite spiel about how there is no "one surgery": you don't just show up for an appointment at the hospital one day, then leave the next morning as another gender. She seemed to get it. *Yes,* I explained frankly, this was a fact about me that I am not necessarily secretive about, but at the same time, it wasn't what my book was about, and I thus wasn't going to be comfortable if it was to be the main focus of our interview and the story. I brought up, by way of example, a few other publications (even a gay one), that had mentioned that I was transgender merely one time, and then proceeded with their review or interview. Again, the reporter seemed to feel me when I explained this, in no uncertain terms stating that all the trans-related stuff we were discussing was off the record, not intended for her story. Perhaps things would've been different, I told her, had it been an in-depth profile, where there's a lot more time and space to at least attempt to approximate a life; but in the space of six hundred words, I believe it is virtually impossible to convey the nuances and complexities of gender identity in any adequate way. And even more so if you don't bring a tape recorder to the interview. Which she did not.

When the piece appeared, I was not super-psyched to see that it began, "So there's this man who used to be a woman, who wrote a novel about a polar bear who comes to Hollywood and becomes best friends with Leonardo DiCaprio." Not great, but if that was to be the reference to my gender identity, then so be it. I kept reading. To spare you the torment of an 85 percent inaccurate and 100 percent snarky fluff piece, I'll just say: in the space of 650 words, this reporter managed to mention my gender identity nine (9) more times.

The most grievous of these: when she described me as having been "a little surfer girl" in my youth. I know this probably doesn't sound like much, but I would never in my life use that term to describe myself. When asked if I surfed and did other ocean-related things when I was a kid, I indeed answered in the affirmative, but I never once used the word *girl* over the course of the interview—not when talking about surfing, not when talking about my youth, never. I don't even say it in real life, outside of a formal interview context. Because it's simply not accurate, doesn't begin to tell the whole story. And it's not a term that feels particularly good, either, like any time I hear the words *she* or *her* in reference to myself. It's all more complicated than that, and I took a lot of time explaining this to the lady, because it seemed like the right thing to do if she was going to be asking about it.

But to call me a "little surfer girl" was not kosher. I just don't think you do an interview with a newly skinny person and constantly bring up how they were obese in their youth, and how everything they do now must relate to that transformation. You don't keep banging that same fat note over and over. Especially when asked not to. You also wouldn't mention ten times in six hundred words if I were physically challenged in some visible way, or had epilepsy. You wouldn't go ten rounds about my race if it was a difficult or fraught aspect of my past; you wouldn't even do it with a gay person anymore—the one punch line over and over to make sure everybody knows: freak! In addition to my gender status, I also happen to be Jewish—and I didn't see the reporter referencing my being Jewish ten times either (she didn't even mention it once).

I am certainly not the first person "of difference" who does not want to be known only for that difference. I am reminded of a time in early 2007 when I did a reading in Los Angeles with the author and poet Chris Abani.[2] We went to coffee after the event, and this subject came up. Chris remembered reading that review of my (then) new novel in the *NYTBR*, wherein the reviewer took time out to tell the reader that I, the author of the book in question, was female. Chris recalled thinking that as odd when he originally came across the review. He told me he was likewise getting tired of reviewers or interviewers insisting upon "reviewing my body" instead of the work. In fact, he was surprised when his physical body *wasn't* the subject of reviews and interviews concerning his body of work.

---

2. Who is black and was born in Nigeria. A fact I never would've mentioned here if it weren't actually relevant to the story. Now I'm going to attempt to resist mentioning it nine more times in the space of this short paragraph.

At a certain point I'm just a man who writes books, advocates for pit bulls, likes both early-twentieth-century jazz and hip-hop, digs old airplanes, has a lovely wife and two kids—and not a transman who is all these things. *Transgender* is a term that implies an identity forever in transition. But I cannot think of a living person who is not in transition to some extent, regardless of gender. That's what we do as humans: we evolve, constantly. Or, as Foucault has suggested, "I don't feel that it is necessary to know exactly what I am. The main interest in life and work is to become someone else that you were not in the beginning."

Dr. Marci Bowers, the rock star of the transgender surgery world whom you see on all the TV shows about the subject, seemed to suggest as much to me when I spent a few days in Trinidad, Colorado, interviewing her for a profile I was writing about her. I didn't completely understand it at the time a few years ago, but I think I'm starting to now. She insisted she was just a woman. Not a transwoman any longer. Not even really transgender. It's just one aspect of your history, being trans, like you were born in California, were orphaned at age eight, or were adopted, had some all-consuming illness, went to Harvard, went vegan, lived abroad, accidentally killed a girl with your father's Oldsmobile. Just one of the many things on the way to becoming the person you are today, man or woman—or anywhere in between. Because every day is filled with transitions, from the tiniest and most insignificant to the largest metamorphosis you can possibly imagine.

I don't want to perpetuate any secrets, and I don't want to straight lie to anybody, but I do sometimes wonder if and when I'll ever just be a man in this world.

A FEW WORDS ABOUT PRONOUNS

WHAT'S THE FIRST THING people ask when a woman is going to have a baby?

Is it a boy or a girl?[1]

Sure, the halfhearted *Is it healthy?* question is usually soon to follow for good measure and/or manners, but mostly folks want to know what the sex of the baby is. Or they don't want to know what the sex of the baby is. All about the sex: *We told the doctor not to tell us! We wanted to be surprised!* Well, I'm here to tell you that gender

---

1. Coincidentally a question I used to hear, often out of the mouths of children, and only in women's public restrooms. This was many years ago, though, when I didn't pass as obviously as male and thus was using about 60% men's and 40% women's restrooms, depending on the seeming safety of the situation.

surprises can happen any time. Just ask my parents.

A few years back, if I had to draw a pyramid to represent who has it "hardest" with respect to the subject of me and pronouns (with "most difficult" on top and "not really difficult at all" on the bottom), it would look something like this:

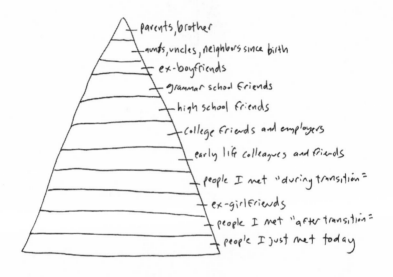

parents, brother
aunts, uncles, neighbors since birth
ex-boyfriends
grammar school friends
high school friends
college friends and employers
early life colleagues and friends
people I met "during transition"
ex-girlfriends
people I met "after transition"
people I just met today

Notice that I am nowhere on the pyramid. This is because for many years, I was generally apologetic about my situation. I didn't want to make anybody feel uncomfortable, ever, so I readily shelved my own discomfort over being referred to by the wrong pronoun. In my early twenties, I had been in a boy band (so being a guy was all just in the name of satirical performance!). And for years after that, I minced around my preference about gender pronouns in real life, splitting the difference, perhaps to make it less jarring for people, asking for no gender pronoun to be used in reference to myself. But that got tricky: "T said T wanted to stop by T's house before we go to bingo."

Closer friends naturally transitioned into calling me "he," which felt best, but when other people messed it up, I was always like, "Whatever! You can even call me 'Asshole' if you'd like— I'm sure it's gotta be really hard for you!" As for my parents, I remember saying to them one time early on, "You don't have to call me 'he' if you can't bring yourself to, but please try not to use 'she.'"

But now I wished I hadn't said any of that. That I'd never spent so much time at that stage. And if I were to draw that pyramid now—again, with easiest on the bottom and hardest at the top—this is what it would look like (most days):

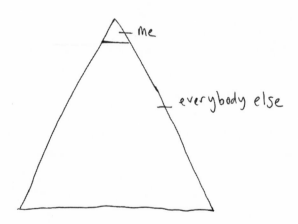

Once I overtly switched to "he" and let people in my life know about it (still in a self-mocking way that let everybody off the hook),

that's when I got off the apologetic train. After fielding scores of "It's so hard, because I've always known you as 'she,'" and "I know it's no big deal for you, but it's really hard for me," I stopped being so goddam accommodating and started gently correcting people, even if it made them mildly uncomfortable in the moment. Because you know what's mildly uncomfortable? Not being seen for who you are, especially by people who are supposed to know and love you. You know what else? People insisting you are something you are not, and likely never have been.

I'm sorry, but I don't understand what's so fucking hard about calling me what I am, what I prefer. If you are introduced to somebody as John, it's not cool to decide to call him Sally, or even David, instead (simply because you choose to, or worse, because you woefully—for John—happen to have knowledge about his past using a different name). Or say you have a good friend you've known for years. You used to go out to bars with this guy, snort drugs, hook up with strippers, and then wake up and do it all over again the next night. If this guy is now five years sober and happily married with two-point-five perfect children, you probably wouldn't call him up every day and ask him to score some coke and go whoring with you. (Especially not if his wife answers the phone.) It's not the world he lives in, even if you think or wish it still is. Maybe it never was him, it never quite fit, and he had to wade through all that crap in order to reach the happy puppies-and-rainbows-filled place he is today.

Or say you always played basketball with a different buddy, that's all you guys did together—played on your high school team, at the

Y, down on the corner, at Chelsea Piers in one of those oppressive adult leagues where everybody has to buy the uniform and celebrate at the sponsoring Irish pub after all the games. But then your buddy is in a gruesome Staten Island Ferry accident, leaving him paralyzed from the waist down, exiled permanently to a wheelchair. Would you forevermore go up to him, see him sitting in that wheelchair, and then be like, "Yo, you wanna go down to the corner and play some pickup? Ooops! I didn't mean to say that! Sorry, it's just so *hard* to get used to!"

No, it's fucking not. You know who it's hard for? The dude who never gets to walk again, never gets to play pickup hoops with his buddies again, never gets to use his dick again for anything outside of involuntarily urinating into a bag. That's who it's hard for.

All these not-quite-right analogies are just a fairly shrill way of saying that it always makes me feel like shit inside when people refer to me as "she." It doesn't happen much anymore (outside family and a few old friends—or the random schmohawk who is introduced to me and naturally takes me for what I look like and what I am, a guy, but then hears from somebody that I'm trans, or does some Googling and figures it out on her own). And it doesn't matter if it's with the best of intentions, or whether it's obvious to those in ear-shot that I am male and nothing's technically been lost, that there's obviously been a mistake. Or even if they are talking about the past.

So as usual, I'll leave it to my unbelievably intuitive and intelligent wife to say it better (and more generously) than I ever could, better than I've personally ever heard anybody—trans or not—put it:

> I think about this sometimes. How I would feel if I were called "sir" while I was on a date, wearing a dress and heels and cherry lipstick. How abnegating it would be to have the world look at you and decide, no matter how many signals you give, that you are something you are not.
>
> There is this misbegotten notion that transmen and women are about playing dress-up and fooling people. But to be trans is to feel the truth so acutely you can't fake it. It is to be so consumed with the truth of who you are that you are willing to risk everything to inhabit it. To refuse to be what other people have decided you are—this is an act of courage few individuals dare try. I know I didn't.[2]

---

2. This is a tiny excerpt from a much larger essay she was asked to write for *O: The Oprah Magazine*, about falling in love with me. I was not identified by name in the piece, though there were a couple photos of us accompanying the essay (wherein we, ironically, look nothing like ourselves).

TEN THINGS PEOPLE ASSUME I MUST UNDERSTAND ABOUT WOMEN BUT ACTUALLY DON'T[1]

1. The physical pain involved in menstruation
2. The emotional pain involved in menstruation
3. How to comment properly on an outfit, hair, shoes, makeup, dress, etc.
4. How much sex is enough sex
5. How completely natural it is to feel one way but then also feel the complete opposite way simultaneously
6. How it feels to be dismissed
7. How stubble feels against softer skin
8. What people think of you if you dare to argue for what you believe

---

1. As my wife has said to me, in the heat of some stupid argument in which I was likely being a dick: "It's astonishing how little you know about women."

9. How certain tasks, by default (or perhaps through the fault of history) tend to fall on women
10. The tyranny of hormones

A BRIEF INTERVIEW
WITH MY WIFE[1]

ME: WHEN YOU FIRST saw that photo of me—before we ever met or you knew who I was, or I knew who you were—what did you think of me? When I tell the story, I always say you just thought I was "some writer guy." Is this close to accurate?

MY WIFE: It is and it isn't. I did think you were a guy. But there was always something else there. Something that made you magnetic in a way I'd never felt before. I don't think this has to do with your being trans (more to do with falling in love), but I suppose, now that you

---

1. Containing far fewer questions than I probably should ask her; there are a lot of questions I'm just not sure I want the answers to yet. Starting with: "Do you sometimes wish I were a 'real' man?"

are asking me to consider it, it could, if only in that something about you radiated infinite possibility.

ME: Do you think everybody who came to our wedding "knew" about me?

MY WIFE: Yes. First, because they were our closest, dearest friends. Second, because information like this travels. It is such a core issue, and it brings up so much inside folks, that I can't imagine it being tamped down. Lastly, it was likely a great comfort to our parents to have a chance to talk about all this complicated (for them) stuff in a safe, understanding place, during one of the most traditional rituals on offer.

ME: Do you believe there's something different about my biology? Like, do you think I may not have the typical XX chromosome setup that those designated as females at birth have?

MY WIFE: That is a good question. I know you are resistant to the biology-is-destiny argument. As am I. But that is probably just stubbornness and ego. Fuck you, genes! I don't care what you say I'm meant to be. An addict, a depressive, slope-chinned, acne-prone, a cheat, a girl. Then you read the medical journals.

ME: How many minutes do I have to be in a public men's restroom before you start picturing me being raped and killed?

MY WIFE: On average, three. Five if I can see the line. Two if we are at a dodgy truck stop.

ME: How many times a day do you worry about something violent happening to me? Is this number compounded by my being trans, or would you worry anyway?

MY WIFE: I worry with every breath. The only time I am not worrying is when my brain is being distracted by other, lesser attentions, like reality TV or my work or what to make for dinner. But the hum of fear is always there, as it is for the children. Sometimes it is manageable. And other times, say after reading the newspaper or another study about girls and rape, or watching something hateful happen on the street, it washes over me how thin the line is between our happy, sweet lives and the moment that could end all of it forever. Because of my experiences and natural inclinations, it isn't challenging for me to imagine the worst. Sure, I would do this no matter what, but the undeniable fact that trans men and women are statistically more likely to suffer myriad abuses doesn't exactly help. Just as having been the victim of violent crime myself doesn't make me inclined to be comfortable releasing my girls into the world. And yet what choice is there? So we truck along, hoping, praying, studying the truth from the corner of our eye. There aren't enough fingers to cross.

ME: List five ways that I am "typically male."

MY WIFE:
1. You are self-involved.
2. You watch TV with your hand down your pants.
3. You never worry about how much you're eating.

4. You get territorial and jealous.
5. You don't apologize for yourself.
Bonus: You spit on the sidewalk.

ME: Are you secretly waiting for a man who's taller, bigger, smarter, richer, tougher, more handsome, more talented, and— most importantly—was born male to come along so you can leave me and run off with him?

MY WIFE: No.

ME: Do you think your mother thinks I'm good for you?

MY WIFE: Yes.

ME: What if one of our kids turned out to be transgender? (For the record, I don't want that to happen.)

MY WIFE: I'll blame you.

ME: How happy are you that this is the last question?

MY WIFE: As if.

BUT WHAT ABOUT THE CHILDREN?

I'VE BEEN THINKING I should probably include something about the children here, perhaps something funny, like when I had to, for the first time, explain the definitions and purposes of periods, cramps, uteruses, ovaries, and vaginas to the girls while the three of us were on an emergency mercy mission to the pharmacy to buy tampons for their mother one rainy night.[1] Or something heartbreakingly sweet, like how soon after I started living with them and my voice wasn't as low as it is now, the older one expressed to me that she wasn't uncomfortable with my being "a different kind of boy," but that her sole concern about it was that she worried that it made me

---

1. "It's not fair you're a boy and don't have to bleed," observed the little one, aged seven at the time.

sad if a waitperson mistakenly called me "she" when we were out to dinner.[2] Or perhaps I could include some sort of sociological observation, like how I noticed early on that being with the kids made me pass more readily and seamlessly than anything else when out in the world—for example in the bubble of Disneyworld, where nobody would ever question that I, even with a voice that didn't entirely match the body at that point, was anything but a real, normal, standard-issue dad, standing in the blazing sun with his wife and kids on line for Big Thunder Mountain.

But you know what? I'm feeling particularly protective of the children, and likely always will, so that's all I'm going to say about them right now.

---

2. To which I responded by explaining that it didn't make me sad at all, that it was completely normal for those mistakes to occur, and that there was nothing for her to worry about or concern herself with. So basically all lies, except the last bit.

TRUCK DRIVER AND HOOKER

ANOTHER GAME, THIS ONE played with my friend J——: It must've been around fifth grade, roughly the ages my kids are now. There was no winning, no object of this game, so I suppose Truck Driver and Hooker should be classified more as "imaginary play" than a game.

We played it in my childhood room, with the door closed, as soon as it grew too dark to roam outside. Details are fuzzy, and I don't remember whose idea it was initially, but the "game" usually started when I would drive up to J—— in a make-believe semi truck and pump my fist two times like I was yanking the horn cord over my head. Then I would roll the window down (manually), coming to a stop in front of her. She would be hanging out on the foot-high carpeted platform on which my mattress rested, fake-filing her nails, bouncing a leg over a knee, pretending to be bored. As soon as I got my window down, she'd eagerly approach my cab, look up at me, and say something like, "Twenty dollars." To which I would either nod my head, "Okay," or—more likely—shake her off gruffly, starting to roll the window back up and pull away in my truck. At which point she would desperately chase after me, suggesting "Fifteen!" or even "Ten!"[1] When I was satisfied with the price, I'd stop the truck, open the door, and indicate that J— should hop in.

I was supposed to have been piloting a sleeper cab, naturally, and what happened next would take place on my bunk in the back of the cab. After I drove off and parked somewhere private (rest area, truck stop?), I would unbuckle my seat belt (safety first!) and tell her to get in the back and lie down on the bunk. Which was in reality just my small bedroom's deep-blue, scratchy carpeted floor, where J— would lie on her back and wait.

The more I try to recall details, the more I feel the entire scene begin to slip away (probably for the best). But I know for certain that what happened next is that I would hold myself horizontally over her, without ever touching her body. Our clothes stayed on, because I had no idea what I was actually supposed to be doing, but I do remember huffs of hot breath and flushed cheeks and a sweaty hand held mere millimeters from her privates, just hovering over

---

1. I guess prices have not changed much since the early 80's, as just recently I was walking alone on St. Mark's Place in the East Village in New York when a methy looking girl came up behind me, told me she liked my jacket, and then got right up in my ear and in a raspy-ass voice offered, "Want a quick hand-job for ten bucks?" (It was nine in the morning.)

her like that. And we'd stay there until my arms would start shaking from keeping the one-arm push-up position for so long. And then I'd roll off her.

And the game was over.

COLLEGE

A Six-Word Memoir

Guys dug me. I mostly declined.

ROCKET MAN

*Another Excerpt from a Draft of the Letter I Eventually Sent My
Parents To Let Them Know I Wasn't Their Daughter Anymore*

...I DON'T REALLY KNOW how to continue to "protect" you from
this information, which is not new and has been floating out there
for a long time. But I can say that some of your past reactions to the
details of my life have colored my willingness to continue to share
those details with you. I take responsibility for my side of that; it has
been a default choice on and off to include only information that I
know will go over without an emotional explosion—it's exhausting
for me to constantly teeter on the edge of disappointment. I'm sure
the denial is equally exhausting to you. As a result it's frequently
been easier for me not to reveal all things to you. To remain in orbit,
intersecting only occasionally so as to leave three quarters of life
out. Like leap year. Because the negative reactions involved (often
to any change, big or small) have included fear, skepticism, and

anxiety—in lieu of things like acceptance or a willingness to try to understand or to be happy because I say I am happy and able to be myself in the world. Life is short, and who knows how much of it is left at any given time. You raised me to be strong and smart enough to know and be myself. Not to live a half life.

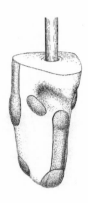

AN INTERVIEW WITH M—,
MY GOOD BUDDY S—'S MOTHER[1]

TC: I'M ASKING YOU these questions because I'm too much of a
wimp to ask my own parents. Or maybe I'm not ready to hear their
answers. Or maybe I'm just being a jerk by not giving them a voice.
They are much improved. They are trying. In fact, things are
fairly normalized now, because I know they love me and ultimately
accept me and don't want to make me unhappy if they can help it.
Not that S—'s and my situations are one and the same, but there

---

1. Names have been obscured. When I asked M— whether she wanted me to
anonymize or pseudonymize names, here's what she said: "I really don't mind you
using our real names, but C— (my husband) thinks we should err on the side of
caution and just use initials, as we don't know where this will be published in the
future, and we do NOT want to end up on *Oprah* or *ET*!"

are of course some fundamental parallels. So here goes: What's your biggest fear about S——'s being transgender?

M——: There have been several fears which have morphed over the years, mostly to do with his being different and the lack of understanding in society. The very first, felt in the anger of initial reaction, was selfish, fear of my *own* social isolation, born of my own insecurity: how S——'s being different would make people think I was "weird" too.

Thankfully, my maternal instincts pushed my selfishness out of the way pretty quickly. My mind then went to protecting my child against people in society who wouldn't accept him. *Boys Don't Cry* came to mind (pretty much all I knew at that time about being transgender), and pictures of Matthew Shepard—the fear of other people harming my child because he was different.

Now that I see how S—— has handled his life and is well accepted by people he meets (he is quite a charmer), I try to leave those fears alone, but occasionally they creep forward. He is quite "out" in his activist job, could be an easy target really, but that's just the way he is. So I have to live with that and accept it, and I push those fears to the back of my mind.

I do realistically worry about the long-term side effects of testosterone. I keep asking him to make sure he takes his calcium every day,[2]

---

2. There is a (fairly plausible) theory that upping testosterone levels puts genetically female bodies into a form of "early menopause," which means that calcium levels drop along with bone marrow density. Even though the presence of testosterone as the dominant hormone in the body should keep bones strong and calcium at levels normal for men of comparable age, some doctors have suggested transmen should

but again this is something we have no control over, and like most medications, the benefits outweigh the risks.

TC: Do you feel like S— is essentially the same person he was before transitioning?

M—: A definitive yes. I would think people might find that hard to believe, and perhaps I would have, too, had I not experienced it, but he truly is the same *essential* being. I think I am fortunate that S— has been able to explain so much to me and is a great communicator. He can express his feelings in the same way he always did. (Who says men can't have a female side?)

I do feel, however, that he has also changed *for the better* because now that he feels at peace with who he is, he is in fact much more self-confident, energized, and productive than he used to be when he wasn't sure of who he was.

TC: When you talk about your child, do you say "daughter" or "son" most of the time? What percentage would you estimate you say "son," and what percentage do you use "daughter"? Do you feel any resentment about having to say "son," because in your mind, you had a daughter for so many years and that is what he will always be to you?

---

nevertheless supplement calcium to defend against the possibility of osteoporosis.

I take a high-quality multivitamin and calcium/magnesium supplement pretty much daily, but occasionally I forget or don't feel like it. Now I think of what S—'s mother said and haven't missed one since.

M——: My husband and I always say and think "son" and "he." It took us about a year of prompting from S—— before we were able to feel comfortable in doing that easily and, yes, I was resentful and angry at first. But as you come to understand what is going on, you see the reason for it and you lose the resentment. Now when we are around old friends who slip into saying "she," it feels entirely wrong and we jump on them to "get with it"!

I think we were helped in this adjustment tremendously, however, since we had to move house from Texas to Philadelphia due to a job change about a year after S——'s transition to begin a "new life" ourselves. We made the conscious decision at that time that we would tell people we had a son and leave it at that.

TC: At what point do you tell people the whole story?

M——: When we get to know people better—mostly because it feels inappropriate to tell people personal details about your life (of any sort) until you judge if you want to share everything with them. There are many people in life that you don't want to get to know any better, yet you still have to work side by side with them, and I just don't feel like explaining everything to such people. Now, as soon as I know I like this person and want them to continue in our lives, then I will tell them the truth. I must be a pretty good judge of character as I have never had a bad reaction.

TC: What helped you most to understand and be at peace with your son's transition? Was there a person you talked to, something you read, a meeting you attended, a morning you woke up and realized something that made you think about things differently?

M——: The first aha moment was pretty early on (about two weeks after his first proclamation), in a heart-to-heart with S——, with him opening his soul to me as to what this meant, how he felt, sobbing from the depths of his being. I knew I had to accept this and deal with it.

It also helped that he brought one of his good FTM friends to stay with us around that time whom I really liked. I never thought of this new person as a "girl," and that helped me to see how it could be for S——.

I had a few sessions of counseling early on, which helped keep me on the right track [with] my "poor me" instincts. I had also been a member of PFLAG for several years (when S—— at first thought he was a lesbian since he was attracted to women). I continued to attend those monthly meetings and found it very helpful to be with other parents who were dealing with having a different child in a society that values sameness.

A further aha moment was when my best friend reminded me of when S—— was four years old, crying out, "But Mommy, I'm a boy, not a girl!" I had clearly denied the importance of this at that time, thinking it was just him being cute and wanting to be the same as his little male friends he always played with, but her reminding me of this showed how deeply rooted this was.

TC: I'm pretty certain my folks are not overjoyed about what I turned out to be. Or, to put it nicer: they would choose something different for me if given even the slightest chance. I don't completely understand the disappointment thing, and sadly (for you), it is falling on your shoulders to clarify it for me. I don't know whether you felt or feel a version of it or not, but a lot of parents of transpeople (and gays too, come to think of it), say that it takes a while to readjust to this new version of their children when they'd been envisioning something else—a poufy white wedding dress, a corner office at Goldman Sachs, or whatever the particular fantasies are. Now that I have children, I can certainly understand wanting as little pain as possible for them, but I don't have a picture in my head about how their lives will turn out, what the specifics will be. I feel like that is for them to decide and discover on their own—and that's the exciting thing about getting to watch them grow up.

M—: You are right, the best parents are the ones who allow their children the freedom to become themselves. However, it's easier said than done, because as a parent you have to take your responsibilities seriously to help guide your child, but where do you stop guiding and just go with the flow? Also, you have to remember that the sexual revolution and the study of psychology were pretty recently introduced just over the last fifty years, which is during the lifetime of most of us parents. When I was getting a degree in psychology and sociology in college in England in the late sixties, homosexuality and transgender issues were discussed under the umbrella of "Deviance in Society," along with the study of the criminal mind. I hope you understand that I am not trying to be unkind here—of course, I shudder when I relate this myself—but that is the reality of what the social norms were back when your parents were growing up.

On a personal level, I don't know why, but I didn't have a clear vision when S— was growing up as to what he would become, so didn't have to deal with a lot of dashed expectations. I was actually quite pleased at times that he acted more like a boy than a girl, as I was a feminist and told my friends he would grow up to be a successful female executive who would have no trouble holding her own with the male power base!

TC: Who was the hardest person to tell about S—'s transition?

M—: It would have been my mother if she had still been alive, but all S—'s grandparents had passed away by then. I think my expectations of what she expected for me and my offspring would have made that difficult—how ridiculous these expectation things are, eh?

If you're lucky, your family accepts you; if you're unlucky, your family bows to society's norms, and there are probably examples of all permutations in between. That older generation (S—'s grandparents) would probably have reacted by saying he had gone too far.

Telling our close family members was pretty easy, as everyone loved S—, and they are all pretty diverse and open-minded. I did sweat sending out a Christmas letter to all of our less close family and friends in England. My husband, C—, actually wrote the letter, as he is braver and more to the point than I am, then I added a few bits here and there. We sent it off and I worried, but we had several people call us with support, and three people wrote lovely long letters/e-mails saying how it didn't matter and how pleased they were that S— had found himself, he was still the lovely child they had all known. We never got any negative feedback and never lost any of our friends.

TC: My parents told somebody they loved and trusted, who has known and loved them (and me) for years, and when he heard, he told them that I had gone too far, and that they were "too old for this shit" and should cut me out of their lives completely. What was the worst response you've gotten to sharing that you have a transgender son?

M—: We are very fortunate we didn't have any reaction like that—I would have felt devastated.

TC: Looking back, did you "know" about S— when he was growing up? What did you "know"? What were the signs, so to speak?

M—: I saw lots of signs, but never thought about his being transgender simply because that word or thought (or the fact that my child was going to be "abnormal" by society's standards) never crossed my mind.

I was always a bit of a tomboy growing up as I had two older brothers whom I played with and emulated, so I thought his boyish attitude was normal. I didn't have expectations for a girly girl—in fact, I am not on the femme end of the spectrum myself, so I was quite happy to have a tomboy child. He was so much fun, curious, outgoing, and intelligent, I was not worried about him being different as a young child. In fact, I celebrated it.

I was worried as he got a bit older—after the age of eight—when the differences became more obvious. For example, when we went away on vacation, he wanted us to call him S— [male name] and pretend he was a boy with the new acquaintances we met there. When we were on vacation at a European resort, he wanted to wear just surfer shorts so he could look like a boy and refused to wear a girl's bathing suit. In Europe people are much more relaxed about children running around half naked, but it would have been a problem in the U.S. When we got back home and he was socializing at school again, he followed the boy-girl norms much more—I guess because of peer pressure—so I figured it would all work out and didn't think anything more about it.

TC: Do you ever feel like S—'s being trans is "your fault"? (I know some parents of transpeople report feeling some version of guilt.) Do you believe being transgender has a biological basis, you know, like Lady Gaga enlightened us, that he was "Born This Way"?

M—: Well, yes, sometimes I do think that since I gave birth to him, I did play some part in how he is. Ha! I am aware of the various theories about what may contribute to being transgender—the difference in certain structures of the brain seems to make sense to me—but that's a scientific explanation of how someone may have developed in a different way. It doesn't explain how that person is the same if not better in so many other ways. Perhaps it's a blessing, not a curse. You know, I can also feel very proud that perhaps his being so smart and wise and lovable is also "my fault"![3]

---

3. Since this interview was conducted, my friend S— has hit a rough patch. When he was younger, before transition, he attempted suicide a couple times. And he did again recently—thankfully unsuccessfully. S— has struggled with depression and anxiety over the years, having things completely under control for long spells, then less so for others. Now, though, he is getting a handle on his condition, and with the help of proper medication and counseling (plus a yogi/swami) is learning to live with his particular challenges. It's a day-to-day struggle, of which his mother, stepfather, and several friends have been extremely supportive. (He is one of the lucky ones in that regard.)

I thought about leaving out this update on S—, so as not to be a complete downer, but at the same time I think it's important to include it, especially in light of a 2010 survey that found that 41 percent of transgender people in the United States have attempted suicide (twenty-five times that of the nontrans population rate). The same study found that 19 percent have been refused medical care because of their gender status, and 2 percent reported having been violently assaulted in a doctor's office.

I have no doubt that discrimination is behind most of these elevated figures, especially when you start adjusting for race, class, education, access to health care, HIV status, homeless status, and a million other things, all of which only compound "minority stress" (which I like to think of as "transie panic," which I definitely have, if only on the days I am reminded of it).

MY MOTHER'S FAULT

WE WERE A PRETTY open family, physically, affectionately. My parents often took naked saunas and Jacuzzis together (not like *that*), as well as with me and my brother, and while my father would generally holler, "Look away!" as he was exiting the water and reaching for a towel to cover himself, I still saw full moons as well as snippets of other stuff some of the time. My mother was naked a lot in front of me (she still is on the rare occasions we're staying in a hotel together over the holidays, or she asks me to talk to her while she's in the bathtub when I'm visiting). My brother was never shy about being nude either (I have a number of vivid memories of him standing buck naked in the garage, fishing through the clothes dryer for clean Levi's, which he would then pull on without any underwear). I, however, recall always being extremely anxious about being naked in front of my family—not to mention anybody else—as a kid.

My preferred swim attire was surf trunks with nothing on top. For years nobody seemed to care or pay much mind to this, until one day on the last day of school/first day of summer—it must've been around fifth or sixth grade—I remember my friend and me getting made fun of at a pool party because we weren't wearing tops with the bottoms of our swim suits. I generally don't have the sharpest memories of childhood (I'm always thinking I'm deficient in some profound way because so many people I know seem to remember every fucking tiny thing that happened to them, while I can scarcely recall where I ate lunch every day in high school or whether we had lockers), but I do have a distinct memory of clinging to the side of the tile drain of Pepperdine University's Olympic-size swimming pool and feeling bad about whatever I'd just overheard the kids saying about me. That's all I remember. And I also have no recollection of how I resolved that bad feeling in my preteen brain, though I did eventually just conform and began covering up—especially by the time I entered puberty (on the late side) and it actually started to matter.

But that is not the point of the interlude. The point of this interlude is to place all of the blame for what I turned into on my mother, who used to tease me when I was being shy and refusing to get naked in front of her.

She'd ask, "Do you have a penis under there?" and fake grab for my towel. "Let me see right now! Are you hiding a penis in there?"

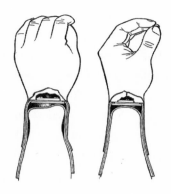

AN INTERVIEW WITH L—,
MY FRIEND C—'S FATHER[1]

TC: WHAT'S YOUR BIGGEST fear about C—'s being transgender?

L—: As a parent, our greatest wish is for C— to be happy and safe. So we worry, a lot. This is further complicated by the fact that we lost our son Christopher, who was robbed and murdered at work when he was eighteen. This is a long, sad story, but it has its consequences concerning our attitude toward safety.

---

1. Names have been obscured. When I asked L— about whether he wanted to use his name, he wrote me this: "I don't know if I want to be anonymous or not. I don't think C— is worried about privacy, but I don't want to end up on *The View* or *Jerry Springer* either."

We worry about the hormonal drugs, the operations. We also worry about C— finding a meaningful relationship with a partner. We worry about marriage and kids and all the possible outcomes and complications. And we fear that real stupid, very evil, and half-crazy people will do bad things for no apparent reason. My son was killed for $300 by a seventeen-year-old kid whom he befriended one night. He said he only meant to stab him and not kill him.

TC: Do you feel like C— is essentially the same person he was before transitioning?

L—: Yes, C— has never really changed much in our eyes. In our case the transition was very, very slow. I can say that I really do not completely understand what actually transpired with the Cherie to C— transition and when. As Cherie, she told me she was gay from the backseat of my car driving home from her apartment on the day Chris was killed. I don't know why she picked that day, but she probably felt things couldn't be much worse, so what the hell! That was almost twenty-one years ago.

While growing up I had no clue of anything gay or transgender. C— was a tomboy, sort of, had boyfriends in high school, but we did not see any more boys when college started. After college C— was still Cherie, living in Provincetown and San Francisco as Cherie—the name change came later, which at first mystified both my wife and me. I was tipped off about the transgender thing by a young woman at work who was once gay, after I had mentioned that Cherie was now calling herself C—. I never even thought about that as a possibility for C—. That was probably about ten years ago or so. I never told my wife [but then] C— told her a few years later. C— also wrote a letter to all family members prior to the operation, which happened a few years ago.

I had a picture taken with me and C— in San Francisco in 2000 that was hanging on my wall in the office. A friend asked me how old my "son" was, and I responded, "That's my daughter, and she would appreciate the compliment," because C— has looked like that always. Nowadays he has a little deeper voice, a little more facial hair, a little older and more strongly built, but really he's the same person. A little less moody and confrontational, but that also could be getting older and wiser. I had a terrible temper until I was over forty, as did my dad.

TC: When you talk about your child, do you say "daughter" or "son" most of the time?

L—: I love this question because we are so screwed up on the he/she, daughter/son thing. My wife and I actually talk about it all the time. My youngest son is great. He changed over like someone threw a switch in his brain. We do not resent saying "he" or "son." It's just so damn hard to get the brain acclimated to it.

TC: On that note, do you tell people you have a "daughter" or "son" straight off? At what point do you tell people the whole story, that you had a daughter, but now you have a son?

L—: We are really screwed up with this also. I've actually had Cherie be my daughter and C— my son in the same conversation, like the kid cell divided or was cloned. But in the case of my son Chris, I made certain rules. In business and most social situations, people ask about your kids. Some to talk about their own, and I just let those people go and tell them I had three kids, two boys and a girl; they accept that and keep talking. It is very difficult to say your son was murdered. Then to tell the actual story, the poor soul you are talking to is just about in tears, and then what do I say? "Oh, by the way, my daughter is transgendered and is now my son." So I really need a script to stick to, and I don't have one as of yet. Sixty-five years old and struggling. Not that I am ashamed or anything, it's just complicated. It's like someone asking, "How are you?" Do you really tell them, or just say, "I'm fine, thanks."

TC: Would you say you are at peace with C—'s transition? (Scale of 1 to 10, with 1 being "cutting him out of your life completely" and 10 being "marching in tranny pride parades.") Will you ever be completely and entirely at peace, do you think?

L—: C— has always been an activist. Really came out of the closet with a bang, with writing and artwork. Traveled thirty to forty cities with [a periodic literary road tour] doing spoken word in every major city including the Deep South. Talk about worrying! For the record, during that period C— was gay, or a least we thought so. So tranny pride parades are kid stuff to us, no problem there.

I think before anyone had a clue about transgender issues, C— appeared on *Jerry Springer* as a woman being male in a background lineup. That had to be around twelve years ago. My wife's very strict and conservative father saw it, and it really upset my wife because we had no idea what it was all about.

We have attended some interesting shows that C— has organized and met some very interesting people. I am one of the few parents who watched a lovely young woman transform onstage from a young girl to a young man, with music and slides, explaining the emotional journey and on to end the show by exposing his female breasts. After the show, we went out to eat, and I sat next to the talented young man with nice breasts and my head didn't explode, but almost....

So we are at peace. I think probably a 9.5 or so.

TC: Who was the hardest person to tell about C—'s transition?

L—: It was hard for my wife when she found out, very confusing for her. I was learning about being transgendered for at least a couple of years before C— officially told us.

We really haven't told many people. The letter C— wrote about it went to a lot of family. I am the oldest of nine kids, and my wife has two sisters. My stepmother and her mother are still alive. No one has really mentioned it. I think it has just become accepted. My family all got together at my sister's last summer and C—, as always, was very outgoing. Most of our friends know and it's accepted, not really discussed.

The tough one is my wife's mother. Not very liberal, is all I can say. It has never been discussed in front of her and never will be.

TC: What's the worst response you've gotten when telling some-body that your son is transgender (or when somebody found out another way)?

L——: We have never had a negative response. But then it seldom comes up in conversation. Maybe it will more often once I get my story straight.

TC: Is there something you might've done differently while C—— was coming up, had you known you were essentially "raising a boy"?

L——: Cherie was born when I was a senior in college. Raising children back then was a little old-fashioned; spanking was still the norm, and smart, independent, headstrong children (like C——) tended to have conflict, especially with my wife, who was raised in a very, very strict environment as opposed to my situation. I was raised in a more open, take-care-of-yourself environment, having lost my mother when I was twelve. So I am not sure life at home was a joy for C——. If I had to do it over again, I certainly would have made sure home life was quite a bit less strict, but then we were rais-ing a daughter. I think we raised Cherie sort of gender-free, except we did treat her with the extra control parents give a daughter and not a son, which C—— rebelled against consistently.

C—— told my grandmother when she was about five, "I am not going to get married; I want to be somebody." C—— wore a dress to school one day in the first grade and that was that, didn't want to do that again. C—— made it to the prom and was class president senior year, and one hell of a catcher on the girls' softball team, and the first kid in town to shave half his hair off and get a nose ring. C— worked at the local deli [at the time], and a woman asked my wife if he had cancer.

It's fair to say we could not be any prouder of C— and his achievements so far in life. Maybe in a few more years I'll have my act together about this transgender thing.[2]

---

2. A couple days after L— shared his thoughts with me, his son C— texted me: "My father sent me his responses to your questions. I have to say it is extremely moving. Our relationship has changed vastly, and the level of introspection from him is huge! There was an implicit request for healing and forgiveness in his responses and his desire to discuss them with me. Thanks for this unexpected side benefit to your project. Love, C—"

THE VIOLENCE CHAPTER

IN MY AND MY wife's heads, it all ends with me getting fastened to and dragged behind a pickup truck. I suppose we stole that from James Byrd Jr. of Jasper, Texas. You remember Mr. Byrd, kidnapped in 1998 by three white supremacists, chained to the back of a truck by the ankles and dragged for two miles on pavement—apparently conscious all the while, until his body slammed into a culvert, severing his right arm and head from the rest of his body. The three guys who did it went to a barbecue after dumping what was left of Byrd's body in a local African-American graveyard.

Then there's college student Matthew Shepard, who was tortured, beaten, and left for dead after being strung up on a fence outside Laramie, Wyoming, that same year. The two guys who killed him at first claimed that Shepard had hit on them in a bar that night, so they naturally flew into a gay panic and pistol-whipped him beyond recognition. The story eventually emerged that they had hatched a scheme beforehand to pretend to be gay in order to rob someone, possibly specifically Shepard, because they thought he was well-off. Either way, Shepard was targeted because he was gay.

And even though his name isn't on the federal hate crimes prevention act like the two men above, rarely very far from my mind is Brandon Teena, a Humboldt, Nebraska, transman who was beaten, raped, and later murdered by his "buddies" in 1993 when they found out he had not been born male. They felt they had been deliberately fooled by Teena, and before raping him, forced Teena to strip naked at a party to prove to his girlfriend that he wasn't a "real" man. Despite Teena's filing a report during the time between the rape and murder, the local police did not find sufficient evidence to arrest the two men who eventually went on to kill Teena and two others in the house where they found him (the rape kit having mysteriously disappeared from the ER).

These three cases helped build momentum to pass hate crimes legislation in the U.S. on both state and federal levels. The Matthew Shepard and James Byrd Jr. Hate Crimes Prevention Act became law when President Barack Obama signed it on October 28, 2009, after being introduced in several forms several times before and *killed* each time. It is the first federal law to extend protection to transgender people, expanding the 1969 federal hate crime law to include crimes motivated by a victim's actual or perceived gender, sexual identity, sexual orientation, gender identity, or disability.[1] It also removes the prerequisite that the victim must be engaged in federally protected activities like voting or attending public school in order for a crime to be considered aggravated by bias (in addition to earmarking funding for investigation into and record keeping of hate crimes).

Though it seems like a no-brainer to get on the books, the reason so many folks opposed the bill and oppose it still is because they feel it limits free speech. That is, you should be allowed to *say* all homosexuals should burn in hell and be sent there sooner rather than later, even if you're not going to *do* anything violent to put them there. It's not just Focus on the Family's James Dobson and Westboro Baptist's Fred Phelps who feel this way. Many of our elected representatives believe these protections are not necessary because we are all supposed to be equally protected under the law already. But more strikingly, opponents of the bill believed that it would prevent religious organizations from expressing their beliefs openly and freely—even though the bill specifically refers to violent *actions*, saying nothing about violent or hateful speech or beliefs. Even so, I'm going to go out on a limb and suggest that the three guys who killed James Byrd Jr. because he was black mightn't have been inspired to carry out such a crime had they not been exposed to suggestive, violent hate speech so often and so thoroughly in the first place. Humans aren't born haters. But of course that veers into "thought crimes" territory, and is thus off-limits.

---

1. It thrills me that the law even knows how to distinguish between sexual identity (who you are attracted to sexually), and gender identity (what gender you are identified with). Now if everybody else could figure that out too.

Violent crimes against trans people are occurring at higher rates than ever. Or maybe it's just being reported more. Or maybe more visibility creates more opportunities for confusion and frustration, which can and often does lead to rage and violence. It doesn't really matter why, but the bottom line is, you can't help but sometimes think about decapitation by culvert, or the tracks Matthew Shepard's tears carved in the crusted blood-and-tissue mess his face had become during the last hours of his conscious life. Or about the stars-and-bars-loving young man who lives down the block from us, and how he looks and acts strikingly like one of the dudes who literally blew Brandon Teena's brains out one night (and then stabbed him afterward to make sure he was really dead, because Teena had been "twitching" after being shot).

So *yeah*, I'm a little edgy. Afraid that I'm putting not only myself, but more importantly, three ladies who love me very much and are invested in my making it home safely every night, in some sort of jeopardy by essentially advertising something that I'm ambivalent about being in the business of selling in the first place.

I guess that's why it's called senseless violence. Nothing makes sense, and right about now it feels like any overarching premise I'd had is starting to sour, the narrative unraveling, this chapter falling apart, paragraphs and sentences decomposing beneath my fingertips. All as the atmosphere around us is growing even more volatile, hateful, and menacing—not less. The untethered fear makes us act in ways and think things we probably shouldn't. Like maybe I should just discreetly live my life and keep my mouth shut so as not to attract any unwanted attention. Be happy with what I have and not act uppity. Don't dress slutty, so you don't look like you're asking for it.

Imagery of these three men's lives intrudes at inconvenient times—or more accurately, their deaths do. When my wife jokes with me before I head into a particularly red-looking bar or truck stop, "See ya, Brandon." Or when a Tennessee state representative goes on the news and threatens to "stomp a mudhole" into any transgender woman who uses a public restroom in his state. ("Stomp a mudhole" refers to beating someone within inches of his or her life.) And federal legislation or not, I don't feel extra protected. Or even nominally protected—forget my special rights! Some days I don't give it a single thought; others I can't get it out of my head. And sometimes I get so frustrated with myself for not being able to get it out of my head, for being afraid—or for not being more afraid. For feeling even a flash of fear or concern, either real or imagined.

Like just the other day, my wife was out to lunch with a newish friend. (We recently moved from a blue state up North to a decidedly conservative and religious one in the South.) The friend is very nice, open-minded, liberal, active politically. Cool. She couldn't wait to talk to my wife about something she'd read when Googling some of my wife's work, the way people do sometimes when they meet a new person and want to find out more about them. We'd been spending some time together as families because of the kids, and all the while, she hadn't "known" about me. Neither had her husband. She'd had no clue! And was surprised (and delighted) to read it. It's so great! They have trans friends at their Unitarian Universalist church (MTFs, but still). And gay friends. All kinds of friends. She LOVES *Middlesex*![2]

---

2. Which is not a book about a transgender character, and it drives me insane when I hear so many transpeople citing it as their all-time favorite. Or when non-trans

She's so happy for us, and even used it as a "teachable moment" about tolerance and difference for her kids (one of whom is in school with my children).

This might seem totally fine. Maybe it is. And her intentions were nothing but good. But in our household, here's where our brains go, pretty instantly: this friend now goes off and mentions us to someone, totally harmlessly, say to a trans church friend, or a gay one. Or just a "regular" one! In any event, she says, in this decidedly small and aggressively religious town in which we now find ourselves most of the year, where we progressive and atheist types downtown find and hang on to one another the way Holly Marshall clings to her daddy whenever dinosaurs come around on *Land of the Lost*, "Oh, you should meet the Coopers, they're a nice new couple in town, both writers. He's *transgender*. They have two kids. They're great, I want to have a party and introduce you."

Harmless, right?

We all do that kind of shit all the time, call people how we see them. The nice new Mexican family down the block. Or the lesbians who bought the pink house with the pool on the corner. Or the white couple who just brought home an adorable baby girl from China. Or the little people with the average-size son in your kid's sixth-grade class... only what I "am" is not readily visible from the outside. It is my past, not necessarily my present, and especially not in an entirely new town with a whole bunch of people who don't know me, didn't know me before, and have no reason

---

people think they really "get" trans people because they've read that novel. I know it shouldn't bother me, but it really does.

to think I'm anything but what they see: the short dude who just moved in with his wife and two kids. A visible man.

It's just plain nobody's business what kind of man beyond that. Or how I grew into one. Just like it's nobody's business if you were molested as a child. Or had an abortion. Or you were the star running back in high school. Were adopted. Had sex with your sister. Survived cancer. Or any number of things that are in people's past (good and bad, but let's be honest, folks most like talking about the bad and different) and completely invisible until they make it your business by sharing.

Of course we cannot control, well, anything in the world, but when the sheer veil of our privacy is not maintained and respected, even in seemingly harmless ways, we can't help but grow reflexively nervous. Not nervous about the people who understand that information is indeed harmless. Of course those folks are not the problem, even if I hadn't yet decided to share with them my history myself. It's those who feel that fact about my past is actually harmful, and even directly threatening to them and their belief systems. *Their way of life!* That, like Brandon Teena's new friends, they've been deliberately hoodwinked. That I've been strutting around like I'm one thing when in fact I am something else entirely. I have taken something that isn't mine for the taking. That I am at very best a liar, but most likely also a pervert and possibly a child molester. Some twisted subset of homosexual.

In some men (and especially small groups of men), this ostensible betrayal has the potential to provoke extraordinary rage and unspeakable violence, you hear about it all the time,[3] and while I am not actively hiding anything or trying to fool anybody—I am living my life as I know how—my very existence is an abomination to some, likely including the church-attending folks who smile and wave at me from their front porches every day as I'm loading my kids into the car, or walking my dogs, or working on the house. And the folks kitty-corner from us who baked a cherry cobbler when we moved in and brought it over as a welcome. Or the ones on the other side of us who didn't have time to bake, so brought over some locally made cupcakes instead.

When the guy who's always smoking on his stoop down the block hears about a man who's not "really" a man or some such, having just moved onto his street, he'll at first think, *No fucking way, it's got to be a different guy than the one I talk motorcycles with.*

---

3. I forgot to mention Angie Zapata, the 18-year-old transwoman in Colorado who began dating and eventually had sex with a man whom she'd met through a mobile social network. After he spotted old photographs of Angie in her apartment, the guy confronted Zapata, who maintained that she was "all woman." At which point, the man grabbed her genitals and then proceeded to beat her to death with a fire extinguisher, until he "killed it," (his words). He was eventually convicted of first degree murder and a bias-motivated crime, after the jury heard taped jailhouse conversations in which the murderer told his new girlfriend that "gay things must die" (see, nobody knows the difference between sexual identity and gender identity, even when sleeping with "one").

It was the first time a state hate crime statute resulted in a conviction in a case involving violence against a transgender victim. And the only sliver of an upside by my thinking is that the murderer will be in prison for the rest of his natural life, with the only sexual contact available to him provided by men (or possibly even other transwomen like Angie, trapped in the purgatory of men's prison due to their genital status).

But then he'll start looking at me differently (while still waving; this is, after all, the South), and eventually he'll put it together. Most people are hip to the gay thing nowadays, but they don't even have wires in their brains to connect the trans thing just yet, and certainly not in their own backyards. So he mentions it to that shifty-looking son who's in his twenties, perpetually primed like a piston, in and out at all hours of the night, and eventually we cross paths on the street some weekend night, me coming home, him just heading out, and he's already drunk with his buddies, or more than drunk, and when he sees me he hisses to himself, or might even say out loud, "Fucking faggot."

And then we're off.

Tyrone Cooper has a lot of outstanding bills. He might've served some time for check kiting, or for credit card fraud. He burns through cell phone companies at an alarming rate, and more than a few ladies have tried to get in touch with him about delinquent (or nonexistent) child support. Over the years, I have been the recipient of a great number of calls pertaining to these and other related matters.

But I am not Tyrone Cooper.

Upward of dozens of calls per week have come in for Tyrone Cooper, on and off for roughly ten years at my residence—until I stopped answering the phone, deactivated voice mail, and removed an answering machine from the line. When I have explained to the various callers that I am not Tyrone Cooper, and that Tyrone Cooper has never lived at this number or address, and that I do not in fact know who he is, nor am I related to him or have ever heard of him... I am rarely believed. I am instead assumed to be covering for

Tyrone, or for myself, or for us both. I have begged to be removed from whatever list my number has been added to, but the calls keep coming, an endless string of dogged, ominously threatening messages pleading for immediate full payment (or a mutually agreeable, adjusted payoff schedule).

I am the kind of person who periodically sits down with a stack of junk mail and actually takes the time to call companies and flintily demand to be removed from their mailing lists, pleading for my privacy to be respected and trees to be spared—often five or six times per company I'll have to ask before I am successfully removed. Or sometimes I am never removed, despite years of calling on my part.[4] So when I get calls for Tyrone, I will swear to the people on the other end of the line, in the most sincere and desperate voice I can conjure, that there is no Tyrone Cooper associated with my address or phone number, even though the computer screen in front of them insists there is. Every other shred of evidence to the contrary. I will offer anything—a signed and notarized letter from my mortgage company, a copy of my photo ID, a fruitcake every year come holiday time—to please stop calling, to stop filling my voice mail to capacity and interrupting my telephone conversations with the click-clicks of call waiting. I promise them, You will never happen to call one day and catch me in a lie, nor will Tyrone by accident pick up the phone and suddenly send in a check to settle all of his outstanding debts.

One night several years ago, I shrieked into the phone so loudly and hostilely:

---

4. Dell computers and Kiehl's being the worst offenders by far.

I AM NOT TYRONE FUCKING COOPER!

that an upstairs neighbor knocked on my door to make sure everything was okay.

A common complaint against trans people goes something like, "Well, I could wake up one morning and decide I'm Marie Antoinette, but that doesn't make me Marie Antoinette, now does it?" People are going to decide what they decide, think what they think, assign whatever identity to me they desire: what they see in front of them at any given time, a perspective that has as many iterations as pairs of eyes taking it in. Like seeing my telephone number on a list and calling my home repeatedly over the course of a decade, insisting I am somebody I am not.

They are among the most private spaces in the world, the periods before and after transition. Not to mention during. And yet it becomes very public very quickly. Because of the goddam social contract, which means that everything you do has the potential to affect everyone around you, everyone you care about, who cares about you. The magic of life (should you choose to engage it). Yet when you do something like this, something so far out of the lines—not to mention off the pages—of the coloring book, people from your own parents to parents of your kids' schoolmates to people who hear about you down the block suddenly have a dog in the fight.

Which I get. If I sincerely believed pit bulls' jaws could lock,[5] I wouldn't want one running loose around my neighborhood. And

---

5. This misconception being almost as absurd as the one about transwomen's seeking to secure unfettered access to women's bathrooms so they can molest little girls in there.

if I believed being transgender was abhorrent, indicative of sickness of the mind and body and moral weakness and poor decision making, it would follow that I wouldn't, for instance, want my kids spending much time with a transgender person. If one of my kids' friends' parents was an active heroin addict—or let's up the ante, say a registered, recovered sex offender—I indeed wouldn't want my child spending the night or much time at all in that person's care. It's not that heroin addicts or crackheads are bad people (though of course child molesters are). They just seem to make some bad decisions that I wouldn't want my children inheriting the consequences of, even for a short time.

People in New York and San Francisco, or Los Angeles for that matter, Berlin, Bangkok, Amsterdam, London[6]—maybe even you, wherever you reside—cannot understand *what the big deal is,* what is at stake when you live in a gender that is different from the one assigned to you at birth. That's because only *everything* is at stake, pretty much all of the time, even if there are long periods when I don't think about it or don't want to think about it or don't even particularly care much about it at all. It will almost always come up some way, internally or externally, benignly or potentially threateningly.

Ultimately, it doesn't really matter who or what I insist I am. The proverbial, If I had a dime for every time I am asked, "What does T stand for?" I would be a rich sonofabitch. "It *has* to stand for *something*." From police officers to sales clerks to credit card

---

6. Hell yeah, I'm generalizing wildly.

companies to airlines, new friends, friends of friends, many of them grow viscerally angry as I repeat, "Nothing. It's just T, no period." They think I'm just being coy. Or a dick.

"NO. What is the NAME on your BIRTH CERTIFICATE? That your PARENTS gave you at BIRTH?" Spoken like I must be simpleminded.

Okay, okay. I understand you think this is your business. So sometimes I will give in: *You got me, I'm lying…* it's really Tommy.

No… Travis (usually at hardware stores and auto repair shops, for some reason). Actually, Theodore (at the public library, dry cleaners, the food co-op, out at bars). Tyler, Tyson, Terrance (food establishments). Toby, Troy, Tim, Todd (random Web sites requiring log-ins).

Tariq (at the airport, once, but never again).

TYRONE.

I swear on my children's lives, it doesn't stand for any of these—or anything else. *Just leave it the fuck alone and call my name when those two goddam medium mango-banana smoothies are ready for my thirsty kids. Thanks.*

"IT"

Part One

SHORTLY AFTER MY WIFE and I got together, a female cousin of hers told my wife that her brother (my wife's other cousin) referred to me as "it" when he heard that my wife was seeing me. He threatened, "If *it* comes anywhere near me, I'll kick *its* ass."

By way of an example of some of the challenges that people of gender difference sometimes encounter in the course of their lives, my wife included these words—without attribution—in the story she was asked to write about our relationship for *O, The Oprah Magazine*. But when the cousin who shared her brother's threat with my wife found out, she grew instantly incensed, even though no identifying descriptions (not to mention names, theirs or ours) were to be included. First she claimed that her brother hadn't meant what he'd said. Then she insisted he'd never said it in the first place, that my wife was remembering incorrectly. Or perhaps even making it up entirely.

"Which was it: did he not mean it, or not say it?" was the only question I wanted to pose to her as I watched the heated exchange between my wife and this female cousin going down over dinner at a burrito joint in New York City one night a few years ago. But I couldn't get a word in, she was that loud and raging, pointing and screaming in my wife's face like you see people doing on *Jersey Shore*, before storming out of the restaurant with her fiancé in tow (and within full view of our perplexed children, who were sitting at a nearby table). I have never, before or since, seen my wife in an altercation like that with another person. It was so volatile and over-the-top that in the moment I assumed the cousin was joking—or that they'd had fights like this all the time (neither was the case; Trannygate 2009 was the first time they'd come to blows about anything).

The one thing I did manage to say to the cousin—after the initial explosion, but before it ratcheted up into the red zone—is that it seemed like she was trying to protect the spewer of those shitty words, rather than standing firm on the fact that she'd thought those words shitty enough to report to my wife in an incredulous, disappointed way in the first place. This cousin prides herself on being an NYC hipster with tons of queer friends, and yet when it was time to come to Jesus, she couldn't do the right thing. I love my own brother and feel a deep and abiding sense of loyalty to him, but I don't necessarily agree with (nor am I proud of) some of the shit that has come out of his mouth over the years. He probably feels the same way about me.

Trannygate took place well before publication of the story, during the editing process, so out of respect for her cousin's apparent second thoughts about having shared her brother's threat, and to minimize any further discomfort on anybody's part, my wife removed any mention of either cousin from the story (even though, again, in the original draft, the guy never could have been identified, as my wife did not use his or his sister's name, nor even her own full name for the piece). Nobody would've known that he was transphobic, that he had threatened to bash me. And nobody else in the family had to be publicly associated with a tranny—or a tranny lover (which was initially a concern for some of them).

Ever since a couple weeks after Trannygate, my wife and her cousin have not been in contact; my wife had to stop returning phone calls and e-mails when the drama became too heightened. Her cousin just didn't seem like she wanted to work it out, even to agree to disagree, to take some space. The two had been extremely tight before the incident—that cousin was one of my wife's closest relatives in the family. She and her fiancé had been guests of ours on a recent weekend; we'd all spent the previous Thanksgiving holiday together at our house.

I feel as though the split is my fault, that *what I am* caused an unprecedented wedge among family. That what I am caused my kids to be exposed to a family member they loved acting so terribly, and worse, treating their mother so abominably—after having shared a perfectly fun day ice-skating at Rockefeller Center, and coming home toting a souvenir snow globe with their photo inside.

I also feel sad for my wife, that after so many years of affinity and trust, she was reminded of how little it takes for someone to turn against you and drop out of your life entirely, to revoke support and even a modicum of kindness or loyalty in favor of somebody clearly in the wrong. Protecting the one with the power instead of the one without it.

"IT"

Part Two

AT ABOUT 9:30 P.M. on April 15, 2010, a twenty-seven-year-old transgender man named Colle Carpenter was allegedly attacked in a men's restroom on the campus of California State University Long Beach, where Carpenter is a graduate student. In the attack, Carpenter reported that his assailant accosted him in the bathroom, referring to him by his first name, and proceeded to push him into a stall, pull his T-shirt over his head and shoulders, and then cut him with some sort of a blade on the chest—perhaps an X-Acto knife—carving the word IT into his skin before fleeing. Carpenter returned to class after the incident, and a professor later took him to the hospital. The assailant has never been found, despite seemingly cooperative efforts of campus security and Long Beach Police Department.

What do you say about this?

Being attacked in a public restroom is one of my most prominent fears. It's sort of like I just assume it's going to happen to me at some point, just something I have to go through, and then it'll be over and I can move on. Not a matter of *if* it's going to happen, but rather *when*—you know, after an agro guy inadvertently spots me through the crack between stalls in a movie theater restroom, or accidentally pushes through a door with a broken lock at a truck stop, and there I am, vulnerable and wiping.

When I heard about the attack over a year after it happened, I wanted to interview Carpenter, so I wrote him a short note through a social networking site, and he wrote me back. He was (understandably) wary of talking about the incident, said he hadn't spoken to anybody about it, though he had received quite a few requests from the media. But he did eventually talk to me, once, for about half an hour on the phone one evening. He spoke throughout most of the conversation, and was fairly candid about his life, his physical challenges (not even related to the attack), and other interpersonal stuff involving his role as a coparent of a young boy, a lecturer who gives "Transgender 101" presentations at various organizations and educational institutions across the state (which is how he believes his attacker knew his name), and as a graduate student in rhetorical theory, focusing on gender performance and the construction of masculinity. I wanted to, but did not, ask specifically about the attack, which he referred to at various times throughout the conversation in roundabout ways.

Before we hung up, I asked Carpenter whether I might send him a few questions to get a dialogue started, and he responded in the affirmative. He said he'd read them over, think about it, and get back to me, either answering my questions or letting me know that he wouldn't be interested in being interviewed.

Here are the questions I sent him right after our phone conversation:

1. How much can you tell me of what happened that night? I haven't read much beyond a few newspaper stories— even though I've imagined it a lot—and anybody who reads this will likely be unfamiliar with what happened, so I was wondering if we could just start off there, with what you're able to say about it...

2. Has there been a day since that you don't think about it? Are there physical reminders of it that you have to process daily (scars, etc.), and if so, do you have any plans to do anything further about them?

3. What did you say to your son? How do you explain something like that to a kid?

4. Have people mostly been supportive of you? Are there any folks who haven't been? I've read and heard about people doubting the attack actually happened, that you made it up. Where do you think that might be coming from?

5. Has what happened ever made you wish you hadn't decided to transition? I know that sounds crazy, or maybe it doesn't, but sometimes, like when I've had to have med-

ical procedures or have been sick and don't know what's going on with my body and have been at the mercy of somebody who has never come across somebody like me but who in that moment is infinitely more powerful than I, there's this really tiny (high) voice in the back of my head going, *You brought this on yourself...* Or when I feel like I'm making life harder on my wife and kids...

But he never responded to them. I sent a couple follow-up e-mails asking whether he'd had a chance to check out the questions, and he wrote back that he had, and was working on answers. He'd just had some difficult life circumstances to deal with, medical issues, social drama, hospitalizations, etc. At one point he asked me to resend the questions (which I did), and told me I could e-mail or call him anytime. But at a certain point it dawned on me I should probably just leave the guy alone. So I did.

The truth is, I realized, he probably couldn't tell me what I really wanted to know. Nor would I have been able to ask.

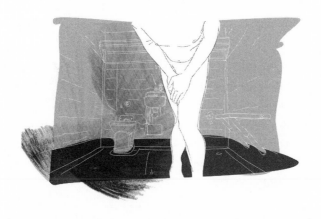

SITZPINKLER[1]

A RECENT STUDY FOUND that about 40% of adult Japanese men sit down on the toilet to urinate (outside of when they are going number two). Larry David makes a strong case for sitting to pee on one of my favorite episodes of the TV show *Curb Your Enthusiasm*, and Muslim men are supposed to sit or squat to pee all the time (something about avoiding impure urine splatter, as Islam strictly prohibits direct contact with urine or feces). Since the subject of sitting down to urinate is something I spend a disproportionate amount of time thinking about, I decided to conduct a study of my own, in which I surveyed 31 of my male-born-male

---

1. A German term meaning "one who sits to urinate," with implied undertones of weakness and being hen-pecked or effeminate.

(adult) friends about their STP (sitting-to-pee vs. standing-to-pee) habits.

21 out of 31, or approximately 68% of the subjects, responded to my query—the 10 deadbeats having obviously decided they were too proper to discuss such matters with me. (I assured all potential subjects that I would be using first names only, should anybody be quoted in the study—and still there was 32% attrition. Thanks, guys: way to really show you care about the advancement of science.)

The results:[2]

- To Japan's 40%, 11 out of 21, or approximately 52% of my homeys[3] said yes, they do sometimes sit to urinate.
- 10 out of 21, or approximately 48%, responded no. A sample of the comments accompanying the no's (most of them decidedly emphatic[4]):

"No. Never ever, so zero percent. Never." —Doug

---

2. I analyzed the data using what little I could recall from a Probability and Statistics course I took senior year in high school, in which the teacher let us watch VHS movies of our choice during class every Friday and most Mondays—because he "just didn't feel like math sometimes."

3. Gay, straight, young and old, and of varying races.

4. Given the slight whiff of macho-with-a-sprinkle-of-gyne-/homophobia implied in some of the HELL NO, I WOULD NEVER BE SUCH A PUSSY AS TO SIT TO PEE–themed responses I received, I was surprised that 30% of the emphatic nos turned out to be from gay subjects, whom I'd thought might be a little more sensitive to the pitfalls of stereotyping. But maybe that just makes me homophobic to be surprised by that.

"Fuck no. Never. And I insist you use my full name."

—Adam Mansbach

"No. And I don't sit down when I'm too drunk to aim well, because that would lead to falling asleep right there." —Alex

"The yogis sit and cut off the flow like a kegel a few times because they think it's good for the prostate. Not me. I did that for a while but missed the sound made from high above." —David

"NO, NEVER. Drunk peeing is fun; I like to make designs and letters and dance peeing. But toilet texting is harder and I'm afraid I may drop the phone in the toilet. Many people who sit to pee find it more productive, so they can use both hands on their mobile devices." —Danny[5]

"No. Only if I am on the phone and don't want the person to know I'm peeing, although sometimes I just piss [while] on the phone and tell them I'm running the water." —Scott S.[6]

"The ONLY time I pee sitting down is if I think I'm throwing a number two, but it's a false alarm." —Munson

---

5. I have no idea what the fuck he's saying.

6. I struggled with whether to put this respondent into the yes or no category. I went with no because upon follow-up, it seemed like peeing while on the phone was a rare situation, and that as he says, sometimes he'll just go ahead and make the noise and then lie about its source.

Of the 52% yeses, I requested that these respondents estimate the percentage of the time they sit to pee. Averaging all of their self-reported sit-to-pee percentages, I found that this segment of my sample sits on the toilet 35.5% of the time.

There was a slight complication with the validity of this figure, as not every fellow reported an exact percentage to me, and some broke down their sitting-to-pee habits by time of day (for instance: "100% during the night, 80% when I get up, then 10% during the day" —Trac[7]) or location ("20%. Only at home or work." —Mo). Others further complicated my analysis with responses like the following, which was very illuminating overall, but not very helpful statistically speaking:

"I will sit to pee in the middle of the night so I don't have to turn on any lights, and when I am at the home of a woman—it's a respect thing because no matter how great a guy's aim may be, there's no hitting the target 100% of the time, and I'm not going to make a female friend clean up any pee I may have missed in my attempts to wipe down the rim (if only guys live at a house, then I stand). The other time I'll sit is after orgasm because the stream is just too unpredictable and all over the place after coming, so why even try to hit the target while standing? When drunk I could usually care less about hitting the target, so unless at a female friend's home (see

---

7. I averaged these and ended up giving him a 63% for the purposes of coming up with the group average.

above), I'll just stand." —Spencer[8]

In addition to the drunk-peeing theme running through the comments (a circumstance I likely telegraphed by suggesting it as a possible reason to sit to pee in the introduction to my survey), I uncovered a few other areas of note. The first, as introduced by Spencer above, is the theme of:

COURTESY TO WOMEN

"40%. When I'm home and it's the middle of the night. Any other time at home, I have to put the seat back down anyway, being the considerate guy that I am, so why not just have a sit?" —Scott C.[9]

"A) When I'm drunk. B) When I get up in the middle of the night. C) When I am the only guy in a private bathroom full of girls at a party." —Madison

And then there's LITERARY/ARTISTIC circumstance:

"4%. I do it to read something short, like a poem in the *New Yorker*." —Jaime

---

8. Two things: 1) After further investigation, I gave him a 35% for the purposes of this survey, and 2) Ladies… this one sounds like a keeper!

9. Who is married, to a woman.

"Rarely. I will sit if there is a good book on the top of the toilet, and I want to read it for a few minutes." —Shannon[10]

"70%. I sit to pee when at my home or someone else's home. I stand when I'm recording music, as I drink a lot of water to keep my voice fresh, and that naturally causes me to pee quite often."
—Andy

"20%. My sitting-to-pee experiences began in my early 40s, along with having to start wearing reading glasses and forgetting to leave the house with stuff I need... like reading glasses; though I like sitting to pee a lot better than those two things." —Mo[11]

"During the day depends on whether it's summer/I'm home/in undies, or whether I'm at work/in tight pants. Easier to take off = easier to sit down to pee. Also, when I arrive, if the seat is down, I sit. If it's up, I don't." —Trac[12]

And finally, of utmost relevance to me and my particular motivations for conducting this study:

---

10. I gave him a 7% because I've been a houseguest of his and witnessed the impressive selection of reading materials kept on the back of his toilet.

11. He is included in the Literary/Artistic category because he mentioned reading glasses, twice.

12. And he's here because he's just so goddam ZEN about it.

PUBLIC vs. PRIVATE RESTROOMS

"30–40%. But NEVER in men's rooms; too many Cro-Mag dudes were never civilized in the art of, 'If you sprinkle when you tinkle, be a sweetie, wipe the seatie.'" —Brent

"Only at home. Never in public restrooms." —Jaime

"I ALWAYS stand when I'm in a public bathroom." —Andy

"100% at home. 0% if I'm in a place of questionable cleanliness such as a public restroom." —Frane

This latter comment I found most revealing and summarizing. It suggests to me a staggering variance in the sitting-to-pee demographic—attesting to just how truly revolting most men's public restrooms are. So in conclusion, as I strongly suspect every time I personally am sitting in a disgusting stall within one, nobody (else) sits down to pee on toilets in men's public restrooms unless he is taking a crap (or thinks he is likely to). Hey, an upside to looking Muslim in the post-9/11 world! What's a little extra harassment at the airport, when I can simultaneously seem completley "normal" in the men's room?

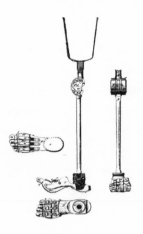

DIAGNOSIS

YOU KNOW THAT PART in *Some Like It Hot* when Jerry (Jack Lemmon) and Joe (Tony Curtis) are disguised as women at a resort in Florida and they spot the gangsters who had been trying to kill them after the St. Valentine's Day massacre? Jerry panics and says, "I tell ya, Joe, they're on to us, and they're gonna line us up against the wall and eh-eh-eh-eh [*sfx: machine gun fire*]! And then the cops are gonna find two dead dames, and they're going to take us to the ladies' morgue. And when they undress us, I tell you, Joe, I'm gonna die of shame."

I have a fairly persistent similar fear: that I will be involved in a tragic motorcycle vs. automobile accident (I'm on the motorcycle), and I will end up smeared across the pavement somewhere someday, and the paramedics will roll up, find me mangled and unconscious, unable to speak or advocate for myself and my physical situation. I'll be bleeding from essentially everywhere, my ulnas sticking out of the skin on both my wrists, but the medics will end up stabilizing me enough to scoop me up and load me into an ambulance and rush me to the nearest trauma center, where en route, the one sitting in the back with me will finally have a minute to go through my wallet, to retrieve my name and other details, and determine whether there's anything about allergies or next of kin or in-case-of-emergency do this or that in my personal effects. He will find my license, photos of my family, my health insurance card, a condom (kidding!), and nothing will appear out of the ordinary—just an unfortunate guy in his late thirties who will be lucky to live, much less walk or talk again, depending on how the next twenty-four hours of his life go.

When we arrive at the ER, I'll be transferred from stretcher to bed, and the instant I bounce onto plastic, the hospital trauma team will begin fluttering around me, each contributing a singular yet vital facet of the process of working me up and hopefully saving my life. A crude incision will be made, a chest tube stuck in and threaded between ribs, another tube jammed down my trachea, CBC, electrolytes, EKG. A nurse will then begin swiftly but deftly cutting my jeans up one leg and down the other, and she will rip them off of me, and they will be bloody and torn at both knees and they will drop heavily to the floor. And then she will proceed to cut my boxers (or maybe boxer briefs that day) in a similar manner, perhaps slightly more gingerly with the scissors now, and tear them off too.... And then just like at Jerry's imaginary morgue in *Some Like It Hot* (except the opposite), my heroic trauma team of experts will momentarily suspend their intricate ballet, because the nurse will look up, nod back down, and at once everybody will NOT see exactly what they THOUGHT they would see on the helpless bloody guy now lying naked in front of them.

And then, if I'm not already dead from my injuries, I will die of shame.

Nobody who knows me will at this critical juncture be there to speak for me. Nobody will be able to replace or supplement whatever thought each of those medical workers has in his or her head in the moment after my boxers come off, about what might or might not be relevant to my health and survival, about what kind of person I am, about the fact that I have the most lovely and beautiful wife and children waiting for me at home—that I have everything to live for despite the fact that my body doesn't necessarily sit squarely with what everybody in the room might've learned in medical or nursing school. And that latter fact will eclipse just about everything else.

Because—and there is no more essential truth than this—the foremost thing on people's minds when confronted with a transgender man is his *dick*.

Peen.

Schlong.

Tool.

Peter.

Pecker.

Member.

Dipstick.

Dong.

Man muscle.

Skin flute.

Chub.

One-eyed snake.

Mr. Happy.

Mr. Winky.

Tube steak.

Beef bayonet.

Baby arm.

Baldheaded yogurt slinger.

Purple-headed soldier.

Ol' one eye.

Baloney pony.

Meat puppet.

Hot beef injection.

Donut puncher.

Pork sword.

Heat-seeking moisture missile.

Main vein.

Jack-in-the-box.

Stinky pickle.

Wedding tackle.

Tyrone Jr.

The reality is, transmen have a wide variety of situations going on "down there." It is infinitely easier to put a fully functional vagina where a penis was, as opposed to the reverse surgery, but a relatively small (and growing) number of transmen do opt to have full phalloplasties, forged out of flesh and skin harvested from their own arms, legs, other sites. A slightly larger number of transmen opt for other various types of lower surgeries that work with what they've already got going on down there. Some just want a urethral-lengthening procedure that allows them to stand to pee. But in my experience, the largest segment of transmen opt for no lower surgery at all (as America learned when Oprah had the "Pregnant Man" on her talk show, testosterone makes many FTM's clitorises grow quite large over time—essentially a size comparable to the smaller end of the male-born-male penis spectrum); they are happy with just top surgery, or none at all. Like everybody else, trans-people do their lives the way that makes them feel most comfortable. And that is all I'm going to say about the topic, having confirmed or denied NOTHING about Tyrone Jr.

One time I got a tick bite, right where the sun don't shine, in a thigh fold—no, lower, *closer in*. Because I had contracted Lyme disease years before, and because I was still in Lyme tick country, and because my wife was able to remove the tick only partially from the bite and it was not healing, I went to the local ER to have someone experienced in such things take a look at my by-then infected bite area.

I checked in, gave them my ID, my insurance card. Waited. Got called in, waited some more. A nurse took my vitals: all good. Waited still more, in the middle of an empty row of chairs beside the nurse's station. After a while a young doctor came over, casually taking one of the seats beside me and flipping through my chart: "What seems to be the problem, Mr. Cooper?"

I told him the basics. He said he needed to take a look. I said it was located in an "embarrassing" spot. He said there was nothing that could possibly embarrass him. I hesitated. He found a free room, we went in, he pulled the curtain; I bent over, pulling down my boxers just far enough for him to see the wound, cupped some fabric in a palm between my legs while he examined me. He got up real close, picked at the bite, pulled a little something out of the skin, likely whatever was left of the tick's head, then suggested I should probably take an antibiotic, prescribed me one, and sent me on my way.

In this instance I decided I didn't necessarily need to "come out" to the doctor about my gender status. I was just going to have to be whatever he, a medical professional, saw in front of him. And even after I bent over and he studied me closely, he was none the wiser. It was still "Mr. Cooper" this, "Mr. Cooper" that. (Believe me, you can tell when somebody has suddenly "learned" something—and this wasn't one of those times.)

But there are other times in the medical sphere when it would be irresponsible (not to mention unwise) of me not to disclose my unique physical situation. By way of example: not too long ago, as I was driving upstate from New York City on the Taconic Parkway, I suddenly got chills, my whole body vibrating out of control. Acute back and stomach pain. Head throbbing. I could scarcely see the road ahead of me. I pushed through for about an hour more of this, driving at least twenty-five miles over the speed limit the whole way, my condition steadily declining, all the while dreading the psychic—forget the physical—discomfort I knew would be awaiting me at the small regional emergency room I was trying to make it to. This time when I entered the ER (the same one I had visited with the tick bite, in fact), I was doubly fretful, as I had no clue as to what was going on with my body. I just knew it was likely not good.

At intake my temperature was 104 and I was starting to grow delirious. I called my wife to see if she could come meet me, since it looked like I was going to be there for a while—but it was the evening, and she couldn't find anybody to watch our kids last-minute. For the time being, I was on my own. In my delirium I started to envision the worst (something akin to my go-to motorcycle-meets-car scenario above). When I was brought into the ER and given a room, I tried desperately not to close my eyes, not to fall asleep or be otherwise unconscious for even a few seconds. A CBC showed that my white count was alarmingly high; even an army of younger white cells was out in force, trying to knock out whatever was fucking with my system. I had a significant infection, but the doctor didn't know where it was. More testing, intravenous drip, and a little something to bring the fever down (they didn't want to administer antibiotics until they knew what was going on). My lower back and practically all of my muscles were killing me; I couldn't stop shivering no matter how many blankets the nurses brought.

I don't have any use for sharing much more detail about my health, but I can say there were minor complicating factors, some stuff I had recently been tested and treated for that might or might not have had something to do with my condition (plus some garden-variety stress on the side). So I knew I had to tell the doctor about all of it. And I mean *all* of it. And he had to tell a couple nurses, and even though I had asked for discretion and sensitivity, had asked that the door be closed when I was delivering the relevant information while the nerdy information dude was typing everything I said into his computer on wheels, it was completely unnerving and humiliating, and I could sense it as the information spread fast throughout the ER with each new person who came into my room to do something.

Not to sound like a baby, but the worst part was probably having to give "the talk" without my wife present. To educate someone who'd literally never treated a patient like me before, even if he'd read a little about it in a medical journal once. To use words like "in this population" and "you can imagine this is a sensitive subject." To be on my best model-minority behavior—while I was feeling my worst. (Just when it seemed like the doctors and nurses thought I was making her up entirely, my wife called to say she'd finally found someone to sit on the couch while the kids slept, and she was on her way, arriving in time to accompany me to the CT scan. SEE, I TOLD YOU: I'M NORMAL AND NONTHREATENING AND DESERVING OF YOUR EMPATHY BECAUSE THIS NICE LADY CAME TO MY BEDSIDE.)

I am lucky, likely because of my class, my race, my education, and ability to—even in the worst of times—sound like I'm not crazy. But I have heard of medical encounters, both emergent and routine, going horribly for transpeople. I have heard of doctors letting their personal feelings about transgender people get in the way of treating them. I have heard of their recording conditions in a way that insurance—if any is carried in the first place—gets canceled, things deemed pre-existing that aren't. I have heard, though it's getting more rare, of transpeople being forcibly put on psych holds and admitted against their will, of transpeople not receiving adequate care and treatment, their basic rights not only as patients but also as humans violated.

It would be nice not to be terrified of falling ill all the time, nice not to have to fly to a New York City clinic every time I need to see a doctor. I mean, being sick and at the mercy of others to make you feel better is already harrowing enough, of course; it might also be nice not to have to worry about all of the things most people who walk into an ER or doctor's office take for granted: that you are presenting with something that your health care professional has likely read about in textbooks, has seen in a class, actually encountered on a rotation or two. It might also be nice not to worry about losing my insurance, nor coming up with the money for costly procedures and medications not ultimately covered because "The diagnosis submitted on this claim is incompatible with the patient's gender," as I have read a few times on paperwork sent my way (including some that came in after the above visit to the ER—it was a kidney infection, by the way, which cleared up after a night of intravenous antibiotics, followed by a few weeks of oral ones).

In countries with some form of socialized medicine, like Germany, Sweden, the Netherlands, and Canada, among so many others, medical treatment for transgender individuals is covered— everything from surgeries and hormones to standard health care for both the routine and abnormal circumstances that arise over the course of human lives.[1] I'm not saying those systems are

---

1. Did you know that doctors in Iran of all places perform more sexual reassignment surgeries than anywhere else in the world (besides Thailand)? I know, crazy, right? In a country of no homosexuals! Actually, the reason there are so many transsexuals is likely correlated to how illegal it is to be gay in that particular country—that is, a lot of gay men (fewer, if any lesbians) transition in order to avoid a punishment of death for committing homosexual acts. And the Iranian government gives them money to do it, and makes it rather simple to change all documentation such as birth certificates and IDs.

Imagine being born male, and when you become sexual you find yourself so

always perfect. (Some require patients to essentially "go all the way" in order to benefit fully from state-covered services. That is, you could not, as a transman, say, elect to have top surgery but choose not to remove your uterus or eventually have some sort of genital procedure.) That being said, in these countries, there are ample places to seek medical care where you don't have to feel like a freak, where you don't have to be afraid of saying the wrong thing, where people have seen thousands of others like you. Where you don't feel like you have to march your pretty, "normal" wife into your hospital room because it actually does put everybody at ease.

In the U.S., transpeople must get notarized permission letters from therapists for surgical procedures such as breast enlargement or reduction even if they want to pay for the procedure entirely out of their own pockets. The exact same surgeries regular old people can wake up one morning and decide they want and then go schedule, transpeople must visit therapists for a considerable amount of time to prove that they are not crazy for wanting to cut off their tits, or for wanting bigger ones. Across this country, non-trans women can pay doctors to attend to their lips, chins, cheeks, eyes, noses, necks, thighs, stomachs, and more, as many times as their bodies and pocketbooks will allow. They can walk into a plastic surgeon's office and get the largest boobs on record put in,

---

attracted to men that you are forced to transition into a female in order to be with men legally in your country. To make yourself heterosexual through surgically changing your gender. I want to write an entire book about *that*.

I mean, so big they cannot walk without seizing back pain that will then require subsequent surgeries to put in incrementally smaller implants… but they do not need letters from psychologists saying they are not crazy to want to do all these things and more. On one plastic surgery TV show I saw years ago, a lady tried to convince a surgeon to implant a giant fucking GEM STONE beneath the skin in her forearm, because she wanted to have it with her always— and nobody asked her whether she might have some other issues she might consider "unpacking" in therapy before embarking upon her THIRTY-FOURTH PLASTIC SURGERY PROCEDURE. She did not need precertification from a psychologist; she just needed the idea and the money. She had *run out of things to do to her body,* so she invented a surgical procedure and sought a doctor to perform it.

Truthfully, I don't care what people decide to do to their bodies so long as they are of age and not hurting anybody else in the process. And I understand it might be a good idea to live in your preferred gender for a little while before you do something irreversible, like cutting your dick off. But I also think it might be cool for people like me not to have to be considered abnormal or as having a "gender identity disorder" just to exercise the same rights and spend my hard-earned cash like everybody else.

Maybe it will get incrementally better with every ER visit like mine, each health care worker slowly educated on a case-by-case basis. But I don't necessarily want to be the guinea pig every time, terrified of needing something and relying upon the kindness of doctors in order to get it. Because even though they have taken a vow promising otherwise,[2] doctors do not always exhibit kindness, or even indifference. (Several years ago, a primary care physician in New York City was in the process of examining me for a sinus infection or something, and about halfway through the exam, per routine, he asked me to lie down and lift up my shirt. At which point the hair on my stomach and chest was revealed and he visibly blanched, stopped talking to me, and immediately retrieved latex gloves and put them on before continuing the clipped exam and hurrying me out of his office with what turned out to be the wrong prescription.)

I hate feeling embarrassed by and apologetic for the paradox of my existence. With doctors is the *only* time I am afraid to continue on the path I've chosen. I want to be the boy in the bubble.

---

2. "I will remember that there is art to medicine as well as science, and that warmth, sympathy, and understanding may outweigh the surgeon's knife or the chemist's drug" (from the modern version of the Hippocratic Oath).

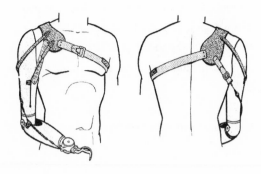

AN INTERVIEW WITH MY BROTHER

ME: WHAT'S ONE OF your strongest memories of me? I'm going to guess it's the story of when I was about two and tried to stab you with a scuba diving knife. Or was it an abalone knife? And did I really try to stab you? Did you really kick me across the room? And why was I holding an unsheathed knife in the first place?

MY BROTHER: Yes! That is it. I don't know why that is such a strong memory, but it is. The way I remember it is we were fighting over something, and there was an abalone iron of mine that you picked up. You were crazy, really mad, and I could see you were way out of control, even for me, and you came at me with it over your head when I was lying on the floor, so I just push-kicked you. I think I nailed you on your chest and you went flying into the closet door.

I also remember a time when you stabbed me with a pencil in my thigh but I don't think I did anything that time. I think we both just stood there looking at the pencil sticking out of me. I was surprised that a pencil was sticking out of me, and I think you were surprised that you did it.

ME: Do you really—in complete honesty—think I was trying to kill you?

MY BROTHER: Thinking back, no. I just saw something in your eyes that told me you didn't know what you were doing. You used to get so mad sometimes.

ME: Here's one of my strongest memories of you from when we were kids: You were spear-fishing in front of the house, and I was tagging along. I was on the sand, and you were out in the water, and then you came in and there was blood all over your foot and ankle. You had been tracking a fish while floating on the surface and when it swam under you and you released the spear toward it, your foot got in the way and the spear went through your heel, like in between your Achilles tendon and the bone. Did this really happen, or I should say, do you remember this incident? And if it did happen, is my memory of it somewhat close to yours?

MY BROTHER: Well, you're correct about where the spear went through my foot, but this is how it happened. I was spear-fishing off the big rock with a spear I had made from a wooden broomstick or dowel. I had attached a steel three-prong frog sticker tip I had gotten from the hardware store, and a rubber sling on the other end. I was using the old yellow long board that Dad got for me at a garage sale on the road when I was around ten, I think. Anyway, when I was paddling in and got to shore into about knee-deep water, I put the surfboard under my right arm and the sling part of the spear around my right wrist and started to walk out of the water. I was hit by a large wave and knocked down on my right side. One of the prongs with a barb on it stuck me on the inside of my heel where you remembered correctly, but the spear was lying on the sand with the surfboard trapped between me and the spear. Every time I tried to get up I couldn't because the spear was holding me down with the board on top of it. That's all I remember. I don't really know how I got out of that mess with the waves hitting me and all, but I do remember that I had to really work that barb around for a while before I could get it out. It hurt like hell.

ME: Do you think about being adopted often? How often? Every day? Once a week? When does it come up? Did you think about it more when you were younger?

MY BROTHER: I don't think about it at all now, but I remember when I was about sixteen I had a long talk about it with Mom and Dad. I don't really remember what my issue was, but I remember I was having issues. I also had a talk with them about eight years ago about my biological parents because I needed to know about inherited medical issues. At the time I was having heart problems and had some plaque in my heart and the doctors wanted to know if I had a history of that in the family.

ME: Do you think the fact that you were adopted and older and I was biological and younger has made a difference over the years as far as how we were raised, how Mom and Dad treated us?

MY BROTHER: No. At least I don't think it was an issue with me. I think you always felt that they liked me over you, but I think you were wrong.

ME: Do you know how I found out you were adopted? Our cousins were in town visiting, playing with me on my bed, and one of them, I think it was —, was like, "S— is so cute, I want to marry him," and I was like, "You can't marry him, he's your cousin," and she was like, "No he's not. He's not even your real brother." I was really upset and cried. Mom and Dad said they told me that you were adopted a lot before, but I guess things sink in when they sink in with kids. Do you remember when you realized you were adopted? Did Mom and Dad tell you, and what do you remember of that?

MY BROTHER: I never knew that happened to you. — was such a bitch. She still is, I think. As far as what I remember or when they told me, I have no specific memory of it. It's like I just always remembered that I knew it. I think they started telling me about it very, very young. The story they tell now is that when they told me I said to them, "You mean that you stole someone else's baby?" I don't remember saying that, I was too young.

ME: Did you want to find your birth parents ever for non-health-related reasons?

MY BROTHER: No. Other than medical history, it doesn't really matter to me.

ME: What do you know about them? Mom told me one thing about the time she almost met your birth mother at a hotel in downtown L.A. or something. She didn't end up talking to her face-to-face, maybe just Aunt Ricki and Dad did. Do you know this story, have you heard it? Maybe I imagined it.

MY BROTHER: Wow! I never knew that. They never said anything to me about it.

ME: How do you think your being adopted affects how you feel about your daughter not getting to know that you're her birth father? Do you think she'll ever learn that you're her biological dad?

MY BROTHER: That one I think about a lot. I mean at least five times a day. I think it's a very different thing to be adopted as opposed to [my daughter] M—'s situation. M— will learn one day soon that I am her real father and that I was lied to about her existence. I don't want her to think that I was part of any of the deception she had to endure. I want her to know I loved her from the day I saw her for the first time, and I never gave up trying to be in her life.

ME: Do you think you'll have more kids?

MY BROTHER: I would like to, but at the rate I'm going and considering the issues I have with trust, I really don't know if I ever will. I think about it every day.

ME: Now that I have two (step)children, I'm seeing firsthand what it's like to raise kids who aren't related to you biologically. I'm not sure I could feel more for them or that I could be more influential in their lives if I were actually related to them biologically. But then again, I don't have my own biological kids, so I have nothing to compare to. I think maybe you can't know unless you have both adopted and biological children, like Mom and Dad—or Brad and Angelina. Have you ever asked them (Mom and Dad, not Brad and Angelina) if they felt a difference in their feelings toward you and me?

MY BROTHER: Actually, I did have a talk with them about you and me. I don't remember when, but it was when we were kids and always fighting; I think I wasn't even nine years old. I had issues because I needed more attention, I guess. They sat me down and told me that they loved us both the same and that I couldn't have all the attention and I needed to try to understand. I doubt I understood but it was something that I would have figured out eventually with a little age.

ME: We used to call you King Jesus. Well, we still do sometimes. Do you think that title was earned at all?

MY BROTHER: I suppose it was, but I really can't pinpoint it.

ME: Do you think we would've been closer growing up if we had been less than seven and a half years apart in age?

MY BROTHER: That's a good question. I think because we had different interests and friends that we never could be as close as we could have been if we were just a few years apart.

ME: Would you say you were a happy kid?

MY BROTHER: Yeah, I think so. Although I definitely would change a few of the choices I made.

ME: Would you say I was?

MY BROTHER: I think you were. I'm probably wrong, though, since you are asking the question.

ME: Did you ever walk in on Mom and Dad having sex? I don't think I ever did.

MY BROTHER: Thank God, I never did either.

ME: Would you say I've "been there" for you over the years?

MY BROTHER: Yes and no. I never really come to you with any of my problems, so how could you be there for me? On the other hand, when I did come to you with an issue, then I would say definitely yes. What comes to mind is the M— thing. You were the first person I went to and you were there for me. I never said thank you. So, thank you.

ME: Ain't no thing. Would you say you've "been there" for me?

MY BROTHER: Probably not. Partly because I don't think you ever needed or came to me with anything, but I would be there if you did. By the way, the few times you have confided in me, I've always honored your wishes and never told Mom or Dad.

ME: How many times have you actually thought about killing yourself? I was scared you were going to do that when I was younger. Was that an empty concern of mine?

MY BROTHER: I don't think I was ever really serious. Just a silly young boy. I view killing oneself as cowardice.

ME: Remember when you picked me up from middle school one day? I think it was when Gammy was dying in the hospital. [Your girlfriend at the time] Lisa was in the car, too. I think you took me to Westwood or something. Do you remember that day at all? I just have an image of me leaning between the two front seats and us waiting on Wilshire to turn left onto Veteran. I don't remember much else—except that you never picked me up from school, so it was a different day for some reason.

MY BROTHER: I honestly don't remember any of that. I do remember sitting next to Gammy in the hospital and holding her hand. The next day she died, but we weren't there.

ME: That makes me sad. I wanted to be like you very much when we were younger. Did you know that?

MY BROTHER: Really? I didn't know that. I didn't think you liked the same stuff that I did.

ME: Why do you think we don't talk a lot now? Do you think that if we lived in the same city we'd see each other more than we talk now?

MY BROTHER: I don't know exactly why, but I would like to see and talk to you more. I just get the feeling you don't want to and have other things to do. Maybe I'm guilty of that too. I think if we lived closer we would make time, but ultimately I have no good excuse. Actually I'm a bit of a recluse and don't talk to anyone much. It's not just you.

ME: What's the most fucked-up thing you remember from childhood? I always think about your friend Shane who died when he snorted rat poison, thinking it was cocaine. What did you think when that was happening, when he was dying in front of you? And when he initially offered you the powder to snort, too, why didn't you do it? (I've never, not once, tried any drug that you snort because of that incident.) Do you ever think about him and that moment when you guys found the stuff?

MY BROTHER: I don't know what I was thinking when that happened. All I remember is that I was scared, scared for Shane, myself, and I didn't fully understand what was happening. I don't know why I didn't do it. I used to think about him a lot for about ten years after that, but I don't really think about it much now. Mostly I would think what his life would've been like if he hadn't died, and if he would've had a family. I never really thought about what would have happened if I'd tried it because I know what would've happened—I would've died, like him. So I didn't try it and I didn't die. That's about the extent of it. I'm really glad you never tried that shit. No one needs any more monkeys on his back than life already gives us.

ME: Were there some ways growing up that I was more like a brother than a sister?

MY BROTHER: No, not really. But then again you're the only sibling I have ever grown up with, and if you've always felt like you were male in gender then I suppose I wouldn't know how it would be to grow up with a sister.

ME: What's your biggest fear about me being transgender?

MY BROTHER: There are only two issues I have, but I'm not sure I would call them fears. The first is, that you are going to screw up your body with the hormones and will end up with a trade-off of a shorter life than you would have not taking them. The second is, you have or will get to a point where the change is irreversible, and then at some point you will come to the conclusion that you have made the wrong decision.

ME: Did it help you to talk to [my close friend] T— about it at my wedding?

MY BROTHER: Yes, it did. In a way I felt like she had a deeper understanding of what you are going through. We did talk a bit privately about you, and she helped me understand how important it was for me to refer to you as my brother, and use "he" when I talked to people at the wedding. I did make the rare and occasional "she" mistake, but if T— was near me, she would correct me with a stink-eye or sometimes a swift smack in the shoulder.

ME: Do you feel like who I am essentially is the same, or different since I started going by "he"?

MY BROTHER: [*Left blank*]

ME: Who do you think is more of a disappointment to Mom and Dad: me or you?

MY BROTHER: I don't think either one of us is a disappointment to them in any way. I will say that I think they might be more disheartened at how my life has turned out than yours has.

ME: Have you ever picked up a transgender suspect in the course of your job?[1] Where did you hold her (or him), in male or female sections of jail or the precinct or whatever it's called?

MY BROTHER: Actually it's unusual if I don't arrest at least one transgender a month. I come in contact with them almost on a daily basis. Where they go in the jail system depends on if they have completed the sex change. In our department males get housed with males, and females with females. It doesn't matter what they were "before," only what they are now.

Trannies and gays[2] are a little different, in that if they're all made up with makeup and dresses and stuff, we usually keep them away from straights for their own safety. The only required question we ask them is if they are straight, gay, or bi. We put them with like others, so they don't get raped or beaten up. If they eventually go to state prison, they aren't allowed to wear makeup and are housed with other like genders. Again, the transgender in prison are housed depending on if they have complete sex changes. It's really not a big deal at all from what I have seen. I have arrested a few males that have had really nice big boobies installed, but they still have a penis. These guys usually are housed by themselves, as you can imagine what would happen if they were put in general population. I don't know for sure how they house them in

---

1. My brother is an officer with the Los Angeles Police Department.

2. By "trannies and gays" I'm pretty sure he means hyper-effeminate males and cross-dressers, or what some people refer to as "transvestites," that is, people who are not transsexual FTMs or MTFs. I think he might even include drag queens in this group.

state prison, but if they have a penis they probably go with other males.

ME: I would imagine you've heard some pretty awful shit said about transgender people while on the job. How does it make you feel when people say stuff like that, knowing you're related to one?

MY BROTHER: "Awful shit" is pretty subjective. The things I hear when talking with people about it have never been what I would consider bad at all. Then again it's not like I go around asking people about it either. Ninety-nine percent of the time it's usually, "Why would someone change what they were born with?" or "Why would you change what God gave you?" I have never had anyone really say anything shitty or mean about it. Usually I get the feeling they feel pity for someone who is unhappy in the body they were born with. However, most of the people I have talked about this with have been other cops.

ME: How do you think Mom and Dad handle what I turned out to be? I didn't tell them for a long time (I think I actually told you and Aunt Ricki first), because I just didn't want to deal, and I thought it would freak them out beyond repair. But they're handling it pretty well now, from my perspective. What do you think?

MY BROTHER: I think they have the same two concerns I mentioned above. Other than that, I believe their biggest issue now is that they think you want them to dismiss our memories and history of your childhood up to the point you made the gender change. We know it is a concern for you, and not a problem for people who never knew you in your childhood, but it is going to be almost impossible to expect us to dismiss or not recognize the great times our family had when we were kids. We feel the expectation is that you want to forget about it because maybe it was a miserable time in your life. If it was, you hid it well and we didn't know.[3]

---

3. (Oh, how I debated whether or not to stick a footnote here. Looks like I did... My book: my rules!) For fuck's sake, I do not want or expect anybody to alter their memories of the past, with or without me in it. Just because I wish to be referred to as male later in life as an adult doesn't mean that my entire early life has been eclipsed. The truth is, I probably wouldn't erase or change much about my past at all. I'm probably one of the lucky ones; that is, I wasn't miserable my whole early life, feeling born in the wrong body, blah blah blah. I'm not saying it was always easy—of course it wasn't—but I am saying that you can remember the past, talk about the past, even celebrate the past, yet still remain respectful of somebody's all-grown-up, new and improved wishes and present-life situation.

People can and should have their own memories, just like I have mine. But if I looked a certain way to you in those memories, if you have decided I was something in your memories, just understand that that is your constructed experience, not necessarily mine. I don't really understand why memories have to be gendered anyway, why they are threatened because I am different now than I was in memories then. I'm the same person, the same soul; I just went through some changes. All people change as they age.

If you want to tell my kids a story about me when I was a kid—like when I got in trouble for writing a letter full of curse words (really bad ones) and putting it in Libby Sparks' mailbox eight doors down, or how I could never learn to spell *beacause* [sic] or *fasion* [sic]—then by all means, go ahead and tell them. They'll love it. Just try to use my preferred gender marker, he, which is what I am. I don't think those stories—or any stories, really—depend entirely on my perceived gender at the time.

And one more thing while I'm on a tear: My choices are not meant to be an affront to anybody else. In fact, they're not about anybody else. People can keep their memories of me and don't have to change anything about them. But if folks wish to be respectful of me and in my life nowadays, then they should refer to me as what I am when they talk about me, up and down the timeline of life. It's really

ME: You don't have to tell me the content, but have our parents talked about me a lot with you? They used to talk to me a lot when they were worried about you.

MY BROTHER: Yes, they have, but most of the time it was regarding how sad they were. Sad not because of your change, but because they felt you hated them. *Hate* is maybe too severe a word, maybe *resent* is a better word.

ME: Do you tell people you have a brother, or a sister, if it comes up?

MY BROTHER: It does come up sometimes. I am not one to hide, and I am not embarrassed of my family or who I am or where I come from. I tell it like it is. If I'm asked, I tell people I have a sister by birth, and now I have a brother.

ME: What, in your opinion, makes a man?

MY BROTHER: The ability and desire to work your ass off for a woman until you're dead, or until she finds someone better than you. Seriously, though, a man is just like any other animal, and it boils down to this: a man has a penis and it is used to procreate his species by fertilizing a woman's egg. The stronger and smarter, the more likely he is to attract a female mate that will bear children to

---

pretty simple. And if it's not, refer back to "A Few Words About Pronouns" on page 53. And if it's still not, then I don't really know what else to say.

care for him when he is too old to care for himself. The stronger and smarter man will have more success ensuring his children's safety, thus becoming more attractive to a woman.

ME: What about a woman?

MY BROTHER: The ability and desire to marry a man who can afford what she believes her lifestyle is worth. Okay, the serious answer is an ability to bear children. The more traits a woman has to successfully bear children, the more attractive she will be to a man. I know you're probably looking for a deeper answer, but this is what I feel to be true. I know these theories have evolved, and you may say they don't apply in today's day and age, however I think the only thing that has changed is that now when we say we are "attracted" to someone we use words like *trust, stability, kindness, good looks, character,* and others to describe what all boils down to procreation.

As far as *love* is concerned, I think it's just a human word to describe a deep trust in your mate that we can't describe in any one word, so we call it love. Not everyone feels the need to procreate these days, as we have evolved a little from the basic animal, but most can find a mate that they say they love.

Before you ask me about people who are attracted to the same sex or transgender, I'll tell you that I am not firm on any one theory, however I'm leaning toward the idea that just like in nature where animals have been documented having sex with the same gender, humans can do the same. And just like in animals the majority of the population will choose to have sex with the opposite sex, and a minority will go the other way. As far as transgender goes, I'm sure there are animals that wish they were born a different gender, but so far only humans have the ability to actually change this. I'm not sure, but I don't think in the animal world you get your ass kicked or are an outcast if you're caught having sex with the same-gender animal like humans do.

ME: Would you rather be a garbage man or a pest control worker?

MY BROTHER: I am a garbage man already. It's just the garbage I pick up happens to be human. To more directly answer your question, I think I would want to be a garbage man because I hate spiders.

ME: What's worse, being adopted or being transgender?

MY BROTHER: Well, I don't know. I don't consider either a bad thing at all. I had no choice in my adoption, and I suppose it's the same with you.

THE THIN BLUE LINE

DEXTER WARD IS A forty-eight-year-old officer with the Los Angeles Police Department. He works as an instructor at the Police Academy, where my brother also worked as an instructor for some time. Ward transitioned from female to male while on the job, beginning his transition in 2004. My brother put me in touch with him about a couple years ago, and I reached out to him, thinking I could maybe interview him for a magazine story. But I didn't really know what to ask of him until I began contemplating this book. Here's what he had to say when we ultimately started corresponding:

TC: My brother said that from his perspective in the department, your transition was handled pretty well by both your superiors and your fellow officers. Is that true? I've heard some horror stories out there in a lot of fields—not just law enforcement and military—so why do you think it went so well for you in the LAPD?

DW: The LAPD has been great. I have had no issues at all. They protect me and come to me for my opinion about trans issues. I have nothing but praise for the department. As for the reason my transition has gone so well, I have to give the credit to [at the time] Lieutenant MacArthur [now Assistant Chief MacArthur]. When we had a big meeting and the department was trying to figure out how they should handle [my situation], she just said that every other company around the country has to deal with this type of issue, too, so let's not do anything and play it by ear, and see what happens and check in with him (me) every now and then. So that's how it has been.

TC: Did you work with my brother directly? How did you get to know each other?

DW: I do not work with S— anymore. He moved on, and I am still an instructor at the Academy, where we worked Tactics together for a while. We had two S—'s in the unit, and he was known as "Blond S—." He was the first person I told, and he was cool with it—he is the most honest guy you will ever meet.

TC: My brother is pretty much the opposite of a blond. How'd he get that nickname—is it because he prefers blondes or something?

DW: Okay, S— is a great guy, but not the coldest beer in the fridge sometimes. Since we had the two S—'s, and your brother was a bit flighty at times, he was referred to as Blond S—.

TC: Well, I think that your talking to Blond S— about your transition really helped him understand and accept me more. So thank you for that. Did he tell you he has a trans brother? If so, when, and how did that go down?

DW: He was kind of not wanting to violate your privacy and seemed very protective of you, so I had to pull it out of him. But I got the gist of what he was asking, so I gave him my information because it was S—, and he is a good guy. I don't remember when he asked because I have CRS (Can't Remember Shit).

TC: My brother also said that one day you were just there in the men's locker room and showers, changing like everybody else. What the hell was that like? Were guys cool with it?

DW: The Friday before I moved into the locker room was when all the captains in the department were notified that a person was transitioning from female to male, but they did not release my name. The following Monday my sergeant was waiting for me outside, so when I drove up he helped me move from the female locker room to the men's. Then we had a unit meeting that same day, and I told the unit that if they had any questions, I would answer [them]. If there was a problem, I never heard anything; you would have to ask S— about that.

TC: Did any of your colleagues or superiors give you shit or a hard time?

DW: There was one guy I talked to all the time about Harleys and stuff, and once I transitioned he would not give me the time of day. I didn't care, since you can't change people's personal opinions.

There was also an instructor who is an ass anyway, and he kept calling me "she." I told him it is "he," and he responded, "Yeah, whatever you are." So I had to take him outside and talk to him. I could have made a complaint, but I found it a waste of my time and energy, and told him so. I also told him that I would not prevent anyone else who was standing in the area from [making a complaint] on my behalf. After that he was always trying to kiss my ass, but I had enough friends.

"Big" John McCarthy (who's an Ultimate Fighting Championship referee now) also worked in the unit, and he put out a jar and announced that whoever called me "she," "her," or used my female name had to put a quarter in the jar. We [eventually] had enough to have a barbecue, so it was very cool.

TC: Can you give an example of a really positive experience with regard to your transition at work?

DW: I am a guest speaker when they teach the recruits the LGBT part of "Human Relations." I like doing that, because after seeing me around the academy teaching, the recruits are pretty surprised when they find out [I'm transgender], and after that they just ask a lot of questions. I have been doing that for the last six years.

TC: Can you tell me a little about the process of picking up trans-gender suspects? When you bring them to jail or the precinct, where do you house them, according to what gender?

DW: If the officers have a suspect who is transgender, they have all been trained on how to handle situations dealing with the trans community. It is part of the "Human Relations" lesson plan. I know people think the LAPD are these big racist police officers, but I have done lectures all over involving trans issues and how other agencies should go about training their officers, and trust me, I would be afraid in any law enforcement agency outside of L.A. County.

I tell a story in my presentation about a trans woman in Memphis who was beaten in the police station, and nobody helped her. [The officers] tried to cover it up, and when the video tape of the whole incident got out, she was going to sue the department, but then she was found in an alley with a bullet in the back of her head. Those officers are still working.

TC: Do all of your colleagues know you are trans?

DW: Some do, some don't. I am not stealth, so if they ask I tell them the truth, but it's a nonissue. I have been in the division for twelve years, and I transitioned almost eight years ago, and people I work with don't care, and neither do the new people. I do not mean to sound like a dick, so I apologize if it comes across like it, it's just no one really cares that I used to be female. I still get the occasional question here and there, but it's not an issue.

TC: Do any suspects ever know?

DW: No, and why would they need to?

TC: Yeah, I guess that's a dumb question...

DW: We also have a trans woman on the job. She transitioned and then joined the LAPD, and the department has kept her name and everything else private. She's [completely] stealth; I don't even know who she is.

TC: You transitioned into, like, America's most hated (a black male), while I transitioned into essentially America's most loved (a white male—though to be honest people generally think I'm Middle Eastern or Puerto Rican). At any rate, in what ways has this changed how you are perceived on the job? Is it different from how you are perceived in civilian clothes, like, just as a black man walking into a convenience store or down the street?

DW: I had prepared everything in my life for my transition, and I do mean everything—except the being a black man thing. You are right: I am now the most hated and feared, and racism is alive and well, and it truly sucks. When you come to L.A. I will have to tell you about all of it. The black man was not always the "angry black man"; just shit around him caused him to be angry.

TC: When I come to L.A. we are not going to waste time talking about depressing racism and angry black men. We are going to spend our time with you whipping my ass into shape in the gym so I can one day be as giant as you are.

DW: Ha, yeah. But I love to eat, so we can discuss workouts over lunch or dinner.

TC: How has your "other" family (of origin) handled your transition?

DW: It was a nonissue. I am the oldest kid and I take care of my mom. I have one sister, four brothers, and six adopted little brothers, and not even my dad, who lives in Texas and is a Jehovah's Witness, has objected to the new me.

TC: Are there things female officers aren't allowed to do, but that you are allowed to do now after transition?

DW: No. All officers are Blue. Gender is not a factor. Your badge says "Police Officer." (Back in the old days of the LAPD, the badges said "Police Woman" and "Police Man.")

TC: What are you doing in the department now, and what are your plans for the future?

DW: I'm still an instructor at the Police Academy, and I am in nursing school during my off hours. I am due to retire [from the department] in about three and a half years, but that doesn't mean I am necessarily going to retire. It's just nice to be able to say that. I want to be a RN and move up to the transman holy land of Washington State.

TC: Can I use your full name, —Dexter Ward, for the book?

DW: I would prefer you to use just Dexter Ward; it's like being stealth, but not really.

TC: I hear that.

MY NUMBER

It's *FRIDAY NIGHT LIGHTS* country where we live now. In the late summer and fall you can often hear the nearby high school band out practicing on the football field during school days, and then cranking it up a few notches every other Friday night from their corner of the stands during home games. The improbably upbeat cheerleaders. The old guy with the young-sounding voice announcing the game over a jacked-up PA system, punctuated by the referees' whistles. The occasional cheer from the crowd, volume regulated by whatever wind's blowing that night. When I give the dogs their last walk on Friday evenings, I always take them to this spot just before our street drops off down the hill toward the high school, where I can see a slice of bleachers through the trees, a bright halo of haze above it all.

So one weekend I decide to take my girls to a game, their first, on the first day of fall, just the three of us. Montessori kids through and through, they have never experienced anything quite like it, don't really know what to expect, reflexively eschewing competition of any kind as they do. They are both tired and resistant. One is leery of the crowd (she's not a fan of loud noises generally), the other just this side of too cool for everything. But the moment we step through security and into the lights on the track surrounding the field, they are both game.

There is something for each of us: D—'s eyes snap to the long line of the opposing team's cheerleaders in tight, neat green-and-yellow uniforms, cranking out nonstop, just that side of too-grown-up pelvic gyrations. She loves to dance, can't help but bob her head along with a cheer when she thinks nobody's looking.

M— is hypnotized by the tubas in the rear and the popping of the drums, the chewed-up sticks clicking on rims. But mostly the too-big, too-boxy, too-synthetic, and completely asexual band uniforms, from shiny borrowed dress shoes to vibrating feathers in caps. ("I might like to wear one of those one day," she says after the halftime show winds down and the home team is setting up kick-off.)

And for me there is the game.

Not to sound like a pervert, because I'm not a pervert, really, but in between fielding a barrage of questions from the kids, getting the right amount of ketchup on a burger for one, waiting for a slice of cold pepperoni pizza to arrive for the other (while simultaneously making sure she doesn't snag more than a sip off my highly caffeinated Mello Yello), I am checking out the players on the sidelines. The stuffed and stretched triangles of their jerseys capped off with neck rolls; the rows of dinged-up helmets suspended at thigh level, not-yet-man hands threaded through their face masks; the second- and third-string guys' pads never looking quite right in their pants. The particularly narrow-waisted guys (likely lowerclassmen) standing on the bench in spotless uniforms watching the game over their coaches' and teammates' heads. Many of them my size or smaller, the size I've been pretty much since high school.

By the time we arrive, the home team is up 14–zip, so I don't bother fussing too much with the game; I can't really with the kids there, it has become about something else entirely. I find myself wanting instead to keep them engaged, pointing things out, the intricate placement of the flags lying on the field before the show, the drum major's glittery shirt (how has someone not creamed him for that?), the teenagers smoking and making out beneath all of us on the concrete bleachers. ("You may kiss boys, you may experiment with a vast and wide swath of things," I say to the older one, "But you will NEVER smoke a cigarette, ever. I never did, not even once. You won't either.")

The little one asks about positions and numbers, what I played, and I tell her I would've been a running back, and if not a running back, then possibly a tight end. Or wide receiver. She doesn't know what any of those are, is just starting to figure out which dude gets the ball hiked to him after shouting a flood of nonsensical numbers on the field. And what he does with it after that. She finds it hard to follow the tiny ball with so many other things going on.

When I played with friends throughout my childhood and up to puberty, I often played quarterback, and thus captain, getting to hand-select my team before each game. I was good; football was just kind of my thing, where I felt most adept in my body. My ideal sport. Somewhere there are a few photographs of me playing ball with some buddies during these years—on the playground, on the beach, in the middle of the street until it'd grow too dark to see the ball anymore. In one image that sticks in my head, I am about the age my younger girl is now, and in it I appear pissed off, one hand gripping an end of a blue-and-yellow Nerf ball, the other out to my side, palm up, frustrated about something—a dropped pass, missed tackle (we are on the beach in this particular shot, so no touch or flag rules apply)—or possibly I'm disappointed in myself, for a bad pass. I have regrouped my team, am approaching the line of scrimmage to give it another down, leather tan with scraggly-ass hair, frowning in concentration.

I've always loved football, though I never played on an organized team. Title IX was born the same year I was, so I suppose I could've tried. But I didn't hear about all those "firsts" until it was way past my time to do anything about them: the first girl to play Pop Warner ball in 1974; the first on a varsity team somewhere in New Mexico the following year; various backup punters and guards and special teams members who fought to have rules bent and parents and school boards assuaged, guarantees granted that there would be no whining to authorities if a girl ended up hurt while trying to play with the "big boys."[1] And nowadays they have full-contact girls' and women's football, though I don't think I would've

---

1. Remember future Academy Award winner Helen Hunt starring in a 1983 made-for-TV movie, *Quarterback Princess*, based on the true story of Tami Maida, who QBed her high school team to win the state championship in Oregon in 1981? I do.

played either, had it been an option when I was in school—or even when I was (technically) qualified to do so. Too much like a consolation prize.

"It's like when the gay guy kicked the ball through the middle of the thingies on *Glee*," M— suggests after a kick, trying to follow my repeated explanations of the difference between a punt, a field goal, and an extra point.

"Kind of," I say.

"Why do you know everything if you didn't play?" she asks then, polishing off her burger. "Too short?"

We laugh—the old family standby about my height, how their mother dwarfs me by a good four or five inches, how they will likely do the same in a matter of months (for one), a year or two, tops (for the other).

Our local high school is one of the many "failing" schools of the South, the kind you can request your way out of by citing a dire need for your child to take advantage of something offered at a nonfailing school that is not offered at your failing school. Like German. Or AP classes. Or fewer weapons, kids of color, pregnancies. Less meth. The school has been state champs in football a handful of times, once quite recently. Some kids have gone on to solid careers in college ball, from Division I on down.

I didn't go to the same kind of school, exactly, but I did go to one where sports were vital. Volleyball and soccer dominated my life in high school (in college it was rugby and the study of tae kwon do). I participated in sports year-round in high school, playing in clubs and training camps during off-seasons. I won some Plexiglas student-athlete award endowed by Xerox during my senior year, was also named to the first team all-state and all-league during my junior and senior years, and second team all-league during sopho-more year in volleyball.[2] Our team won a California state champi-onship one of those seasons, came in second during another, I can't remember which was which now. (I do remember driving back from Fresno really bummed some weekend, like suicidally bummed, after missing first place by the narrowest of margins one season. Feeling I could've done better, done more.) In a state where volleyball was at least as important as football, suffice to say high school remains for me a blur of pressure, most likely of the self-imposed persua-sion. Of constantly battling to balance homework with the need for repetition of another sort, for practice. For perfection.

On the way back from the concession stand (for a second time), I notice a few ladies decked out in maroon sitting at a long banquet table adjacent to the stands—team moms and grandmas, parked on folding chairs behind several towering piles of our team's jerseys, separated into home and away colors.

"How much are these?" I ask one of them.

"Ten dollars, hon'. They're the actual jerseys the boys wore in the championship game," the lady says in a contorted drawl, rearranging a tiny bundle of a baby—definitely not her baby—over a shoulder.

I start riffling through the jerseys.

"What number you looking for specifically, sir?" another lady asks. Helpful. Sweet. "We got just about all of 'em."

---

2. Or some configuration of these honors, but all of them at one point or another during my sophomore through senior years.

"I'll know when I see it; I have a lot of lucky numbers," I say, and she laughs as I begin in earnest to scan the shoulder numbers on each shirt, trying not to make too big a mess of the table. I am more drawn to the home jerseys, maroon-and-white, tipped with black, and my kids start getting in on the task of locating just the right one. They keep holding them up to me: "This one!"

"No, get this one! Can I borrow it sometime?"

"It's too big for you."

"So? I'll tie it."

D— holds up 72, my birth year (way too long in the waist), and M— finds 4, Gammy's birthday, the grandmother I had been super bonded with when I was young (way too big). And then there are some other contenders that I will always associate with favorite NFL players: 8 (Troy Aikman), 22 (Emmitt Smith), 84 (Jay Novacek), 34 (Walter Payton), 20 (Barry Sanders), 32 (Marcus Allen). But nothing really sticks out. Until it does. On the bottom of the second pile, the number-12 home jersey, and it is just the right size and length, Goldilocks on the gridiron. I suddenly remember that 12 had always been my jersey number, the one I wore in every sport—even the one where each position has a specific number assigned to it already (rugby).

The kids help me slide the thing out, encourage me to try it on. Which I do, abashedly. But it feels perfect, isn't too torn up, is stained in just a couple places, and, most compellingly, doesn't smell funky. I pull out a ten and hand it to the lady with the baby, whose other hand rests atop an old-fashioned metal cash box.

"I guess he found his lucky number!" the older lady says saucily, rubbing her hands together as if in anticipation of the games that will be taking this football season way down into fall.

I smile and thank them both, then start to take the jersey off, but D— encourages me to leave it on.

"That seems a little sad," I say.

She looks around theatrically; young and old alike are of course sporting all manner of jerseys and T-shirts, jackets and hats, dumpy sweatpants and sweat towels with the home team's name and mascot emblazoned across them.

"It looks good," she adds unironically, making me feel really old. So I shrug, throw my jacket over it, and we three head off to find a perch from which to take in the second half of the game.

I don't mean to sound maudlin, but just then a ragtag riot of maroon-and-black home jerseys retakes the field just on the other side of the chest-high chain-link fence that separates players from crowd, and before I can shut it down, I am caught in a rare flash of regret, nostalgia for what never was—okay, fuck it: I start feeling a little ROBBED of a fucking boyhood in which the perfect number 12 jersey I am now wearing isn't just some bullshit novelty item I bought to support the local high school team's fundraising efforts, but rather something I actually worked my ass off for years in order to earn the privilege of donning. Of dirtying myself.

It is precisely at this point I feel my little girl—the one who will be taller than I in six months if she keeps going at the rate she's going—grab my arm and hold on to it tight as we walk in front of the bleachers, the younger one pulling slightly ahead to scout us some seats. It is, I recognize immediately, one of those few perfect moments you get in life, a moment that punctures time if you let it, and no matter how cheesy or dumb or obvious, or akin to a television commercial for FUCKING ABILIFY it feels like thinking it, there you are, telling yourself, more realization than directive:

You will never forget how this feels.

With both of her arms tight around yours. With her not yet having figured out that moments like these with her dad—in front of hundreds of teenagers on the bleachers (sitting on each other's laps, investigating and comparing lip-piercing infections, every utterance shouted two clicks too loud)—will embarrass her to no end sometime very soon. That this might be one of the last times, if not the last, she reaches for you like that, a kid who needs you and knows she does, reminding you: *dickhead, you would likely never be here on this side of the fence right now, had you ever been over on that one.*

GALLERY (B)[1]

1. All four of the bodies you see in Gallery A and Gallery B belong to transgender men, people who were assigned female at birth, but transitioned into men (I might or might not be one of the four). They're here for three reasons:

    1) My wife sometimes refers to my species—well, me in particular—as a "magical unicorn."

2) In my experience, a good number of transmen are quite comfortable showing their bodies (and their torsos) publicly, on the Internet, in galleries, posing for photographers, etc. In fact, a whole bunch of transpeople, MTFs and FTMs alike, will document every nuance of their transition from beginning to end and beyond online, in photos, videos on YouTube, and various websites dedicated to

sharing information with others who are either undergoing a similar process, or contemplating transition. On sites like Facebook and Myspace (R.I.P.), I've seen guys put up a new photo of themselves every week, so you'll have literally dozens upon dozens of photos of the same person, holding up a camera in the mirror, striking their best pose.

I personally can't think of anything more harrowing (not to mention narcissistic) than having hundreds of photos of myself appearing as self-consciously handsome as possible posted anywhere publicly, but I think I can relate to a constant, seemingly renewable source of wonder on these guys' parts: sometimes you'll catch yourself in the mirror, hear yourself on a voicemail message, or see yourself in a photo, and for one tiny moment, there you are, gob-smacked like the rest of the world is by the improbability of your existence: *That's me? The fuck did this happen?*

On the other hand, there's a whole other contingent of transguys who, wishing to live stealthily in the world, resent when fellow transmen show their bodies—specifically the scars on their chests—publicly like I'm doing here. This is because they believe that the more "regular" people know what torsos belonging to transmen who've had top surgery look like, the less opportunity for those wanting to live stealthily to do so effectively. I used to think that argument so hysterical and even preposterous, like, How could you possibly think you can hide something like that? Dude, wear a wife-beater until the scars fade or something! I've even heard about some stealth transguys answering the occasional benign question, "What happened to your chest?" with, "I had lung surgery," and leaving it at that. Yeah, it was real fucking preposterous and hysterical, right up until the time I heard those exact words spontaneously spewing from my own mouth when confronted with the same question at a swimming pool in Florida one bright and sunny afternoon.

3) There's still this messed-up part of me—and perhaps this entire book is evidence of it—that wants to scream, *Amazing*, right?! I know, we look just like "real" men, don't we?! Anybody would be confused! You'd never know! You see: we really are men. We are really masculine. In fact, a number of us actually reflect a rather narrow, though widely recognized and decidedly mainstream version of masculinity. We could be pledging Sigma Chi, or sweating there next to you in the steam room at Equinox. Hell, the gays even go for us—and who's a more dependable arbiter of masculinity than a horny homo?

HAIKU

Side by side like kin
You would kill me if you knew
Mine's bigger than yours

THE FIRST 48

THERE'S THIS TERRIBLE OIL painting by an unknown artist hanging in our TV room, and when my wife and I have a (usually ridiculous) fight, I sometimes find myself alone on the couch late in the evening, staring at the horrible (okay, wonderful) thing. It's a thrift-store find, marked $3.50 in old-timey looking handwriting on the back of the canvas, and it was probably painted in the forties or fifties, but it is seemingly set a little earlier, during Prohibition. Just this man and his kid, both clad in denim and standing in front of two harnessed and blinkered Clydesdale horses with a farm and silo in the background. The man holds a jug of what I'm assuming is moonshine, his blocky hands just about to uncork it, eyes drifting lovingly down at the jug, while his tiny son gazes up at his father with some sort of admiration on his face. I *think*. (The artist is not the best with expressions or emotion—or farmhouses, pastures, and mountains. S/he is passable at horses, the muscles in their legs at least.)

There is something dreadfully wrong with the people in the painting. They are proportioned wrong, almost like Eastern Bloc gymnasts, even though they are likely supposed to be in West Virginia or Tennessee or Kentucky. They are practically little people, veritable dwarfs, especially the son. Their faces are just awful, rubbery Kewpie doll–like.

I sit there staring at this scene, lit only by ambient light, the room otherwise dark, TV off for the time being. Everyone else asleep, even the dogs. The old house alternately creaking or completely still. Me of course feeling misunderstood. *Mister* Understood. Pathetic. I can hear the hard drive of the cable box spinning, almost like the swivel of vertebrae on vertebrae in the neck segment of my spinal column. I just sit there staring at the little dwarf kid, his stupid, bright-eyed and hopeful eyebrow arch, and how he's NOT EVEN LOOKING directly at his father, like if you drew a dashed sight line from his pupils, that line would hit the tip of one of the horse's ears, way above the father's head. And he's so tiny and ill-proportioned… what is he standing on? Is he the only one standing atop a rock, while the horses and dad are on solid ground? Or is it a hay bale? If so, why isn't it showing? And if he's in fact that small, then he should be just learning to toddle, not be rendered like a little man with his flippery little hands and WAY TOO SHORT arms and no lips like the girl without a mouth in that *Twilight Zone* episode.

There is just something *wrong* about them, something very *wrong* about this short little boy in particular. Why are his arms so stubby and stuck to his sides, no joints in the elbows? And is that a maroon sash around his waist?

I hate myself so much, staring at the guy with his moonshine and his little dwarf kid adoring him. I hate myself for being complicated. For bringing complications into my wife's life. And the kids'. It's not that she's said anything, but I hate that she has to think about things she never had to think about before. If I were just normal, born what I am, born male or whatever I am, she wouldn't have to be afraid, wouldn't have to think twice about disclosing information that should otherwise be harmless. Wouldn't ever have to feel the opposite of pride, what is it, shame? Ever. Sometimes it gets so tiring for us both, wondering about that extra layer, parsing what people might or might not do when they "find out." Preposterous, but sometimes disclosure tips into danger. Then I hate myself even more for caring what anybody thinks or does. For thinking that I can actually do anything to thwart somebody who truly wishes to do me harm.

Or maybe I just say I wouldn't change anything because I can't change anything. It's not possible, so why waste even a passing thought on it?

Sometimes seeing old photographs of myself brings up rage like the rage that comes on those fight nights on the couch, me alone in the dark beneath that moonshine painting. Or sometimes I don't have any feelings about old photographs at all, feel instead completely removed and apart. Perhaps I should've figured out a few things sooner.

There have been some wasted years.

Or they weren't wasted.

That painting just makes me so *angry*, eats me from the inside, and after about an hour or two of resisting tiptoeing upstairs, waking her up, disturbing her already troubled sleep, and telling her I'm sorry, sorry for all of it, even everything we weren't even fighting about, even things I think I'm "right" and you're "wrong" about, that I'm sorry and I would do anything to make it up to you, to please just touch me and let me touch you right now and don't just sleep/not sleep there clutching that pillow between us, grazing one another only on accident, down near the ankles. Somewhere after resisting this impulse for hours, but before I get so deliriously tired I can't resist anymore is when I reach for the remote and flip it to *The First 48*, which is usually on TV, and if it's not on, then I usually have several episodes of it taped on DVR so I can watch them one after the other on rare nights like these.

The First 48 is undoubtedly a man show. Other man shows include anything about prisons, anything about serial killers, motorcycles, garages, anything about major traumas and treating them in ERs and/or on life-flight helicopters. I don't know a woman who watches *The First 48*. My wife refuses, thinks I very well might have a defect because I can watch it. Because I can even watch the same episode more than once, sometimes three times. As though there's going to be a different outcome to the generally two (but sometimes one) murder cases per show. All senseless, none by accident, ever.

I have always loved shows like these, but *The First 48* is among the best, if not the very best. I am fascinated by that CLICK over to murder, the mechanism it requires, if that's the word for it. When men (and it is 99 percent men) decide to give in to the rage and let it rain down upon another, regardless of consequence. A second in exchange for the rest of one's life. Not to mention somebody else's.

I am filled with so much anger at certain times, or maybe it's more like frustration initially, and the anger is just attendant, but either way I don't know what to do with it sometimes, and it is so unexpected and inexplicable and during this latter part of my "journey" in life there have been a few times when I could *almost* see killing somebody in one of these rages. I don't want or need to go into much detail, but there is a very bad man out there who at one time threatened the safety and well-being of my wife (and children) before I was in their lives. Sometimes I have dreams in which this man has invaded our house while I am away, and when I come home, he is assaulting my wife in our bedroom. I go to the safe and pull out a .38 revolver and then walk back to the bedroom and put the barrel to the side of his head. I tell him to get off of her, and when he doesn't, I calmly pull the trigger. I have no problem doing it in my dream, and I'm not sure I'd have a problem doing it in real life either. I think sometimes it would be worth it, that second in exchange for the rest of my life. It's certainly worth his life, extinguishing him so he cannot menace any of the several women he has plagued, and no doubt will continue to plague, over the years. It almost makes me want to cross paths with him, just to see what it would feel like. What I would do.

On *The First 48*, these perpetrators likewise believe in what they are doing in the moment. I feel their chemistry telling them it's the right thing to do, the only thing to do. Sure, I like the lead-up, the first few hours after one of these guys clicks over and a body is found, neighborhoods are canvased, families are notified then interviewed. But my favorite part of the show is once the homicide detectives get suspects into interrogation rooms. It is one of the most compellingly intimate moments between humans that I can think of. Sometimes guys will just crumble, they will want to get it off their chests like the detectives are telling them they should. *Yes, you can have a lawyer, of course you can and should, but I think you might feel better if you tell me your side of the story first, man.* These guys who have just ruthlessly murdered another human being or a handful of human beings merely hours before will just fucking disintegrate wet-toilet-paper-like before your eyes, will cry and blubber and spell out exactly what they did, how they grabbed the AK, turned off the headlights, turned up the block, got out of the car, and for almost a full minute sprayed the outside of a house belonging to somebody they had beef with, not knowing there were other kids inside, and mothers, daughters—a *family*—and that bullets would travel through THREE SEPARATE ROOMS and lodge in the brain of a kid sleeping in bed way on the other side of the house. Would also kill an eighteen-year-old who just happened to be spending the night on the front couch. But would spare the intended target he was beefing with (who ends up with a bullet merely nicking his calf).

I would be one of these guys; I would crumble because it would feel better to tell my side of the story like they say, and I will say I didn't mean it (now), and that I'm sorry (now), and I don't need a lawyer (now), and you might as well just go ahead and book me.

But then there are these other kinds of guys, guys like the one who drove up to his friend on the street and pulled out a pistol and just shot his friend in the face. He would peel off and his shot friend would lie bleeding in the street, and his sister would come out of their house, and then he'd be dying in his sister's arms, and he'd say to her through a mouthful of blood, "Fat... Fat... Fat... Chris.... Fat...," and he will be essentially delivering a death-bed identification of his assailant. He will say, "Help me," too, over and over, but soon he will die. And still that guy, Fat Chris, who it turns out is not really fat at all, will a few days later sit in that tiny interrogation room in his big jeans and big white T-shirt with a bag of Doritos and three bottles of water on the table in front of him, and he will angrily—like he is really being put out by these detectives—he will sit there and say, *Honestly, I swear to you I promise I have no idea what you are talking about, I wasn't even there,* even though there are five or six witnesses who saw him, saw his gold Chrysler LeBaron at the scene, with gun flash blazing out of the driver's side window. And when he finally concedes he was there but didn't pull the trigger, has no idea who pulled the trigger, it came from behind him, so how was he supposed to know which of the three guys in the backseat of the car it was. And then the detective will be like, *I respect you and what you're saying, but what if I told you that your friend didn't die right away, and he said you were the one who shot him?* And Not-That-Fat Chris will sit back, legs planted wide, cross his arms theatrically, and shake his head and continue to insist it was not him, because he is convinced it was not him, not the him now sitting in front of the officers at least, and he is in fact quite broken up about his friend dying, had no so-called beef with his friend, instead only has beef with the cops who come around and bust up his neighborhood and pick people up for no reason when he's not doing anything wrong.

In *The First 48* there is always the question of *Why*. Of motive. There is rarely an answer, confession or not, conviction or not.

When I am at my angriest, when I feel I could do the most damage, it turns out I am disgusted not with whom- or whatever I'm taking it out on. Surprise! I'm disgusted with myself. And that is why the dwarfy kid in the painting and the murderers on *The First 48* comprise the only company I'm fit for, the only company I deserve, at three in the morning in the dark on the couch, when I should instead be in bed lying next to (and if I'm lucky, holding) the last person I should take anything out on, ever, the same one I was so effectively and inexplicably making cry just a few hours before.

MAN CLUB

THE FIRST RULE OF Man Club is: you do not talk about Man Club.

The second rule of Man Club is: you DO NOT talk about Man Club.

The only requirement for entry into Man Club is: you have a penis. Or look like you have a penis. Because why the fuck wouldn't you?

In Man Club, almost every sentence initially uttered by or to a stranger ends with "man" or "buddy" or "bro." Or, often in large cities with youthful, hip populations, "dude." Like when you're paying for something at a register, the cashier, if a member of Man Club, will hand you your change and receipt while saying, "Thanks, man." Or at the end of a long kayak paddle with a friend, as you're pulling boats out of the water, and another man is there doing the same while waiting for his buddies to return with the trailer, he will holler over, "You want a shot of whiskey to top off your ride, bro?"

In Man Club, if you raise your voice and express anger about something, other members of the club actually pay attention and often respond favorably, even helpfully (when not aggressively). Like, if you are telling a contractor to stop pilfering electricity from an outlet on the side of your house, that it's been two months of it, the utility bill is two hundred dollars higher than it usually is, and you think you've been pretty fucking understanding and accommodating thus far, but when the *fuck* are you going to set up your own goddam power line so you can run your entire construction site off your own utility bill? After this tirade, another member of Man Club who is within earshot will, as you walk away demanding, "Fix it," through a clenched jaw, scamper out of your path and ask, "Do you want me to move my car, man? Is it in your way?" even though his car is not in your way and has nothing to do with what you were yelling about in the first place.

In Man Club, you really do talk about sports with strangers when at a loss for conversation. Like if you are waiting for your wives forever outside the changing room at H&M, and the Yankees are playing, the man next to you will ask the score, like, of course you would know the score, but you don't know the score or even that the Yankees are playing, because you don't really care about the Yankees until the playoffs—and nominally at that, so you diddle around on your smart phone until you find the score so you can dutifully report it back and then discuss what an A-hole A-Rod is and whether he's even worth it.

In Man Club you pretend your wife would be okay with your going to a place called the Mouse's Ear, and as soon as you walk into a place like that—or maybe it's called Panty Raid, or let's be honest, it's called the Cooter Ball—everybody there (everybody NOT a member of Man Club, that is), without fail, calls you "baby" and occasionally "cutie" (even if you're a troll). Like if it's slow and the middle of the afternoon and after one of her dances, the prettiest of the girls—Lisa, a dental insurance salesperson when she's not doing this—will come over to your table, squeeze your shoulder, lean in close, and whisper, "Mind if I sit here? I don't like to sit alone." And you will be overly polite, half stand up, and pull out a chair for her, and you will order yourself a Coke and Lisa a Red Bull (no ice) when the cocktail waitress comes around and prompts you, because you hadn't thought to do it yourself. And then the two of you will sit there in silence, only nominally watching one of the other girls who is presently dancing on the tiny stage in the middle of the mirrored room, where she is working twice as hard as Lisa was, as she is two times less attractive. And you and Lisa, plus the three other (much older) men in the joint, with various girls at their tables, will sit there in the dark and watch and listen and put a few dollars into garters or panties and pretend that it's not completely fucked up that half a dozen girls are taking turns removing their clothes and spreading their legs to reveal their vaginas and assholes to complete strangers. As a privileged member of Man Club in good standing, this is all perfectly normal, merely a logical extension of a rigid hierarchy of which you inhabit the top tier, and if you feel otherwise, if you feel that there is in fact nothing even remotely *sexy* about it, in fact find it more *sad* than *sexy*, then another basic tenet of Man Club states that you do not betray it. So you will keep sitting there beside Lisa, and you will not feel the need to say anything about yourself, although she will eventually, because there is just something about you, tell you how she got into the dental insurance industry, how she fell into stripping, then stopped stripping when she got married, how she started up again as soon as she got separated ("while I'm young and my body's still good"). How she drives two hours to get here because if anybody at work found out she'd be fired, and she will, finally, right before she has to go up onstage again, tell you how she met her husband here at this very table seven years ago—and how one night a few months ago she came home one day after work at the dental insurance company and he and his things were just gone.

In Man Club, you talk about women in a way only members of Man Club talk about women. A handful of "down" straight women[1] and a whole slew of butch lesbians out there think they talk about women with men the way men talk about women with other men, but trust me: men talk about women that way ONLY WITH OTHER MEN. Among these two types of women and members of Man Club there may be a momentary performance of, like, We're so grooving on this funny, mutual understanding we have about women and their crazy peccadilloes. But that is *nothing* like how men actually talk about women with other men. It is something else entirely, it can't quite be named really, because to be frank, it is that deeply embedded in the human condition. But it does have something to

---

1. The kind you've read about in *GQ*, *Esquire*, and *Details* magazines ad nauseam— your best-buddy female friend you can itch your balls around, say "cunt" in front of, and go to hockey games with and (supposedly) don't want to fuck.

do with a baseline, foundational understanding that you are simply a DIFFERENT SPECIES from women, and that alone brings you together no matter what other surface differences may be present, and every man knows exactly what I'm talking about, except maybe obviously and openly gay men, who don't necessarily talk about women the way women are talked about by members of Man Club.

Like when I am doing hours of manual labor in 95-degree humid heat with a hillbilly fellow named Vinton who's helping me build raised beds and stone walls for my wife to plant a garden in our backyard, and Vinton and I are sweeping back and forth across a five-acre, three-foot-high grass-covered field for hours, snakes coiled and ready to strike at any movement, maggots and ant colonies roiling under every rock we overturn, as we locate, excavate, and then haul something like three tons of Paleolithic-era stone chunks of varying sizes and shapes, and at some point the ancient owner of the property drives up in his giant Ford F-250 and agrees to let me pay $200 for all those tons, but first he says, "You might want to run a small load by the home front to make sure the missus is happy before you haul all that stone," and the corner of his lip curls up a little as he sets down on the tailgate of my truck. He has a CHOOSE LIFE specialty license plate with a big smiling infant face affixed to his pickup, I mean, you really have to have some serious feelings about a lady's right to have an abortion to go to the DMV and select the pro-life license plate and pay extra for it and then wait for it to arrive because they usually take a little longer, all those save-the-whatever specialty plates. And he knows from my plates I'm not from around here, and we likely have just about the most divergent political, social, and religious viewpoints two individuals can have, and yet here we are, bonding implicitly over this one area, the biggest area there is in fact, the oldest one on record, so old it's probably illustrated clearly on the walls of Chauvet Cave in France—the one that says we are on top, even though sometimes we pretend not to be on top, like when we run a couple different hues of stone by our wives before we haul it: the purpleish, or the rust-colored ones, dear?

She (we?) went with purpleish.

A CONVERSATION WITH KATE BORNSTEIN, GENDER OUTLAW, SEASONED TRANNY[1]

TC: WHY ARE TRANNIES, across the board, so unbelievably self-involved?

KATE BORNSTEIN: Unlike more respectable "trans people," trannies don't have the sanctioned identities that anchor us to the

---

1. This conversation took place over the course of a few days while Kate was in the throes of final edits on her sixth book, *A Queer and Pleasant Danger: The True Story of a Nice Jewish Boy Who Joins the Church of Scientology and Leaves Twelve Years Later to Become the Lovely Lady She Is Today* (Beacon Press, 2012). Now sixty-four, Kate started her transition in the early eighties and is a widely known and revered gender theorist, author, playwright, and performance artist. We first met shortly after I moved to New York City in 1996, and despite my being a bumbling pipsqueak, we became friends and have been ever since.

culture, so we're tossed about until we discover what the fuck it is within ourselves that can get us seen the way we've always wanted to be seen. That means a whole lot of what-the-fuck-am-I-doing, and even more how-are-they-reacting-to-freaky-me. I'd call that self-involvement. Nu?

TC: Yeah, I guess I would. Do you identify with the phrase "born in the wrong body"?

KB: Not in the least. I like what you say about it.

TC: Oh, yeah, being born in the "right" body? I think I feel that way, and then something demeaning will inevitably happen, and I question everything.

KB: Yup, trannydom is both a blessing and a curse.

TC: If there was as much visibility when you were a kid as there is now about transitioning and transgender people (like, if they had *Dancing with the Stars* on TV, or shit, if they even had TV back then)... No, seriously, do you think you would've transitioned earlier than you did, had there been more information and tools readily available?

KB: Y'know what, I'd like to think I would've transitioned earlier. But it was more than television back then, it was the whole postwar hetero-macho-misogynist-homophobic-racist-anti-Semitic glue that held everything in place. We've only been seriously prying ourselves loose from that for a couple of decades now, at most.

But as a fantasy? Wow, sure, I wish I'd been as brave as Candy Darling and Holly Woodlawn and Tula and International Crysis. They were so beautiful.

TC: Speaking of those ladies, who was your tranny role model? (You were mine, by the way.)

KB: I often consult the ghosts of Doris Fish and 'Tippi'. I got a lot of strength-of-girl from reading books by Caroline Cossey, aka Tula. Sandy Stone put me head over heels in awe and gave me hope that I could be a mad, eccentric artist and survive while doing just that. Marsha Botzer taught me I could still be a lady, but I don't think she calls herself a tranny.

TC: Why do trannies get their panties in such a bunch over the word "tranny"?

KB: Trannies don't. Trans women do. Because they think that people will associate them with those horrible sex workers, and that would cost them their jobs and the respect of their communities. Because they've worked so hard to scrape all the sex and desire off the identity of trans. Because they don't want to be treated with disdain by the masters of theocratic capitalism. Because they've been called that name with terrible anger, been shamed by it too many times, and it really hurts them to hear it.

TC: Haven't we all been up and down the "reappropriate the words of the oppressor" road?

KB: Yup. Still haven't figured out the meta solution to the paradox of hate speech being the same as love speech.

TC: I'm going to bring *transie* back. What do you say?

KB: Nah. You say "transie," I say "tranny," so both our books are then filled with hate speech. We are the most transphobic people on the planet. And maybe we'll change some hearts. Won't that be lovely?

TC: Who's the lady who always used the term *transie*?

KB: Sandy Stone. I've asked her if she invented it. She said, no, that's just what trannies of her generation called each other. Why is it you like that better than *tranny*? Just curious.

TC: I don't really like it better, I just cotton to *transie* because it seems old-fashioned, like what ladies used to call themselves before they even knew what they were. There's something sweet about it, although I'm sure even thinking that makes me a misogynist. Which of course I am.

KB: You think you're a misogynist? I've seen you write misogyny into some of your characters, but I haven't seen you do misogyny. Not that I watch you 24/7. Nah—at best you're a miso-nearly-wanna-be.

TC: I'll take that as a compliment, coming from you.

KB: Everything I can think of about you is a compliment, mister man. Well, most everything.

TC: Back to transition. I think if I had transitioned earlier in life, I'd be more interested in living as stealth as possible. Mostly because it would help me avoid some really uncomfortable moments that have the potential to make me feel really shitty. Do you ever fantasize about living stealthily?

KB: Never with any joy. I did fantasize it, never thought I'd be able to pull it off. I dreaded the constant fear I'd have to face if I tried to do it. But I do live stealth as I walk through the world. AND my father-in-law has known me for fifteen years and doesn't know I'm a tranny. Conversation with him is so boring.

TC: Is he among the twenty million *Dancing with the Stars* viewers? You could talk about that.

KB: He watches the news and Lawrence Welk reruns. If you asked him what *Dancing with the Stars* was, he'd probably tell you it's what angels do. He would never call Chaz Bono an angel.

TC: Is Chaz Bono "good for the trannies"?

KB: At this point in his career, the Chaz Bono phenomenon may be good for some trans people. He's a freak like us, and he's holding his course. He's a freak because he's fat, and that makes him embarrassingly unattractive—no one a respectable person would want to be, no one a respectable person would want to fuck, no one a respectable person would want to be seen with in public. He's a freak because he's a celebrity, and respectable people resent how drawn they are to him. And he's a freak because he's an artist, and that makes him laughable and socially undesirable.

Chaz is a *baby* trans thing. He's swung way over to the boy side of the world, including the icky parts of that gender (no offense, there are icky girl parts too). It's going to take Chaz another five years in the public eye, poor fucker, until he gets the internal head and heart room to figure out for himself who and what he is. That's when he'll be amazingly good for trannies and other trans folk.

TC: Do you really think Chaz Bono is an artist? I can't see really anything he's done that could be considered artistic (besides, perhaps, transitioning, which definitely is an "art")—I feel like he's always just been a child of famous people, coming out, penning memoirs, trying to get reality shows, talk shows, record deals, popping up in the news here and there. I also remember his being a vocal lezzie and spokesperson for this or that (the Human Rights Campaign, when they were blatantly anti-trans, as in: let's get all this more palpable gay and lesbian legislation passed first, and then maybe we'll worry about the freaky trannies later). I'm curious what you mean by "he's an artist."

KB: Okay, this gets down to elitism. I admit I hesitated after I said that he was an artist. I almost changed it to "entertainer." Then I reasoned that entertainers are artists and—as you pointed out—we trannies are gender artists. And there are hunger artists, do you know about them? When I'm deep into my anorexia, I'm a fucking artist—I pull forth bones, I disappear. But it's not entertaining. I wish Kahlil Gibran had tackled art and entertainment in *The Prophet*. You and I need to write a dark version of *The Prophet* together.

TC: Okay, but let me get this dark version of me out first. What is, in the end, going to be "good for the trannies"? Every time I read an article about a transperson in mainstream media, I resist reading the comments, I really try, but then someone will e-mail me a link about how Chaz Bono told *Rolling Stone* magazine that he is "saving up money to buy a penis," and so I'll just glance down at the comments—99.5 percent of which are virulently intolerant and hateful and religious and say things like, "Psychological help would be better than mutilating herself over and over." Part of me is like, "Shut up, dude, keep it to yourself." And the other part is like, "Well, I guess folks need to hear about it, but I'm sure glad it's you and not me."

KB: It is you and me. Life just isn't the same for us, holding identities as trannies. Maybe Chaz is a tranny trying to be a trans person—a lot of trannies do try.

TC: I kind of want to be a trans person.

KB: Well, in my advanced years, I've come to see that it's only when we give up and give in to our inner tricksters that we find ourselves a life worth living. The virulent intolerance and hateful religious condemnation is an inescapable part of living out in front of any cultural curve. Whoops—there I go, being elite again. I get that way with you.

TC: It's not that you're being elite. It's just that you're better than everybody else.

KB: Yeah, yeah, yeah.

TC: Truth is, in light of the often grotesque nature of the online world these days, I'm slightly terrified of publishing this book, and I was for a time considering publishing it under a different name, even though it would've been obvious it's me. Then I hated myself for considering using a different name, felt like a pussy. I know you would never consider doing something like that, but I've never put myself out there—it's of course so different from fiction. Anyway, since I am a self-involved tranny, tell me something to make me feel better about all this.

KB: Freedom's just another word for nothing left to lose.

TC: You texted something to the effect that we are fractured people trying to use our art to put ourselves back together again. In some ways we are all doing that, us writer types. It made me think of Joan Didion, who says she doesn't know what she's thinking about anything until she writes it down. That might be what I'm doing.

So, this is your, what, fourth memoir-ish book? Have you figured yourself out yet/put yourself together? Was there elucidation with each publication?

KB: There's that old saw: we teach what we most need to learn. What the fuck does that say about writing memoir?[2] As trannies and trans people, we put a whole lot of stock into what other people think of us, how they see us, how they treat us, what gender box they put us in. When we write, we get to call all those shots. It's heady.

Have I figured myself out yet? Put myself together? More or less, yeah. I have. I've got the components down, and they're all in the right place in the Rube Goldberg device of who and what I am. But putting ourselves together doesn't take into account the never-ending morphing we do as we move from the gaze of one person to the next—and the never-ending morphing we do as we travel through the nature of our desires. I'm always reassembling myself into something that's easy for people to relate to—and I always do my best to become the object of desire to the people I'm mad for. No, no. I don't always do those things—not when I'm cranky. Or scared. Then I don't give a fuck about what people think they see when they see me. And I get all prickly and resentful of the easy time a lot of people seem to have of it just by being normal, and I think mean thoughts. That rule I wrote in [my last book] *Hello, Cruel World*—"Don't be mean"—yeah, well… we teach what we most need to learn.

---

2. Kind of like how I just wrote a whole book about something I hate talking about?

MY TWENTIES
A Six-Word Memoir

Thank God for Astor Place barbershop.

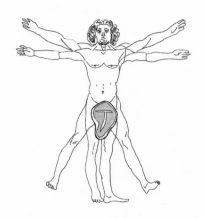

BORN IN THE WRONG BODY

IF IT ALL SOUNDS contradictory, that's because it is.

I think about new money. I think about immigrants. Lady CEOs.

No matter how much you grow, how far you travel, how high you reach—*how deftly you pass*—you will always at least in some small way wonder. You will cut an eye back over your shoulder every now and again. To see who might be coming up from behind, or looking at you funny. You hear Jay-Z do it in some of his songs. Jews do it every day, it eats away at their colons, two thousand years of running and fretting over some form of "The Nazis are in Pasadena."[1] Martha Stewart must do it, too, in a rare flash of

---

1. As my family used to say, given we were living in Southern California.

fragility—perhaps on the darkest of the 150-some-odd nights she spent in the pokey—think, *Do they know what I really am? Can I keep it all up and pull this off?*[2]

I don't care if you are the richest motherfucker on the planet, you came from nothing and now have everything. Sealed away forever are your Midwest trailer park beginnings, and your seventh-grade-educated mom and ninth-grade-educated dad are currently tucked into a luxurious, Scotchgarded, overstuffed sectional in front of satellite TV in the new split-level you quietly purchased in their name within a gated suburban community. TiVoing the *fuck* out of *Dancing with the Stars* and *Two and a Half Men. The Voice*. Making enough Frito pie to freeze and eat for a whole week. You will always harbor a little of that in you.

Or maybe you have done everything possible to shed that, and you don't have it in you at all. There is not a single external indicator, you are instead an Incredible Hulk of a man: five foot ten, thickly bearded, with a Barry White–deep voice, muscles out to here, a don't-fuck-with-me set jaw. I know transmen like this (albeit not green-skinned ones). And on the flipside, I know transwomen who are petite and gorgeous and svelte and delicious in ways that Beverly Hills and Hamptons housewives pay hundreds of thousands of dollars on operating tables in hopes of becoming. NOBODY WOULD EVER SUSPECT! is the go-to, generous compliment nontrans people always give us. I NEVER WOULD'VE KNOWN! had you not told me you weren't born female. Or male. Or poor. Or in another country.

---

2. Not to mention: *Does this knit poncho make me look fat?*

But it's not about what others think you are.

It's what you think you are: what you fear, what you project—even unconsciously, unintentionally. Maybe during one of those moments of weakness. Or in times of illness, or failure. Even if it's the last thing in the world you intend to do. It radiates invisibly, hisses out silently to all but you. But waiting to be confirmed by somebody who is not you.

There are always people who pick up whiffs of something being *off* in others. Just slightly askew. One tick from *normal*. It is not on your person, cannot be discerned from your twenty-five-thousand-dollar pair of sunglasses,[3] the framed Ivy League diplomas on your wall, your bison ranch in Wyoming. Your perfect English. Or that formidable, bulging package you're rocking in your jeans. It's nothing anybody could put a finger on (or five). But it's there. Behind your eyes *beneath* those sunglasses. Or in the way you imperceptibly fix your head like a spaniel, listening and observing for that instant when everything can turn, and you will be exposed for everything you really are. Which is not what you really are, of course it's not. But it's what you *know* most people will forever *think* you are if they ever discovered the TRUTH. And that's why it's contradictory: I'm just living my life and don't give a fuck what anyone thinks—AND—I am TERRIFIED EVERY SECOND of being FOUND OUT.

I don't want to give the wrong impression. I don't sweat every minute of my daily life. It's way more subdued than that. In fact

---

3. "They're, like, four carats of diamonds, and then they're gold python, and they're made of gold… I've got insecurity issues, apparently. Hahahaha!" —Dana Wilkey on *The Real Housewives of Beverly Hills*, season 2, episode 5.

many days I don't think about it at all, not consciously. A lot of the time, I am *most* comfortable with people who "don't know": mooky guys selling me a new set of tires at the garage, tattooed girls fixing me espresso drinks at the coffee shop, old Christian ladies I help with their bags at the grocery. Some dapper gay dude cruising me on Eighth Avenue in Chelsea. I don't sit there through every interaction wondering, WHEN WILL THEY FIND OUT?

You understand? I am at my *best* when the world sees me for what I am, when people assume I am nothing but what they see before them. When every new person I encounter, each new day, is fresh and pure and baggage-free. IN THE MOMENT, as fucking BUDDHIST as it gets. Let go of expectations, control, preconceptions, the past, the future… and there I am in the hardware store, and the cotton-candy-haired old lady ringing me up gives my well-behaved and handsome dog a cookie and says to me with a tear pooling in one eye and the thickest Southern drawl: "You are just the *kindest* and *sweetest* man for adopting a pit bull and helping him be such a good citizen in this world. It's all how the owners raise them.…" It's as though it's the first time a stranger has ever addressed, accepted, and approved of me and my deeply misunderstood and discriminated-against dog, and it feels right. I feel right, even though in truth I feel no different than I've felt all along.

And I am at my most ill at ease when I am, say, sitting around a dinner table over the holidays with my parents,[4] my wife and

4. To be fair, there were two occasions—one in July 2010, the other in December 2011—when my mother stroked my face in a sweet, motherly way and said, "You look so handsome tonight." Which was, if I'm being honest, extremely touching

children, maybe an aunt and uncle, and half a dozen cousins, various spouses. Stories about the past inevitably bubble up, and the hostess is all, "What can I get you to drink, sir" (to me), and the waiter's all, "Are you ready to order, sir?" (again, to me, within earshot of the whole table), and I'm just sitting there, a fairly normal-looking guy with his wife and kids and extended family, and they're all Texan and thus a little bit tipsy and a lot of loud, and I'm giving my kids paper on which to draw exotic fish in hopes of keeping them conscious through dinner because of the time change, and everything looks pretty fucking simple and straightforward, and in some ways it is. But actually it's not, because there I also am, trying to remain present and in the moment, but I'm instead bracing myself against the booth, constantly, anxiously scanning a few seconds ahead in time and wondering, WHEN IS SOMEBODY GOING TO REFER TO ME AS 'SHE'? *Any second now it'll pop out, here it comes...* BOOM! from a cousin, in reference to me: "Remember how she used to always flip the finger in photographs? No wait, that was her brother!" HAHAHAHAHA. And then shortly after, POW! there's the name on my birth certificate, the one I've never really been called, not by my parents, my brother, my friends, EVER IN LIFE, except for official purposes (transcripts and schools and jobs and such), but that magically tumbles out of the mouths of family members now that I've really not been using it for something like twenty-five years. And then for a moment everything in my life feels wrong (if only to me and perhaps, if she's within earshot, my wife), so wrong like

---

and generous, even though I was embarrassed both times (for myself, of course, not her).

it's always been wrong, and there never was any right, even though I still pretty much feel precisely like I've always felt. I'm the same person no matter what people call me. Even the ones who remember the day I was born. Who held me. They of course don't have the power to change what I am, to take anything away, I remind myself. Okay, maybe they do for that second, but then I come right back to level, thinking, *Maybe we just don't spend as much time with family anymore.* Which I promise myself never to do again. That is, until the next wedding or bar mitzvah, or the holidays.

I don't know how many years it will take of me looking how I look, sounding how I sound, being addressed how I am addressed in the world, before some people will use the right pronoun. Or at least not use the wrong one. Maybe it's out of stubbornness, or perhaps they just don't care enough to make the effort or truly understand why they should. I know it's not malicious—they rarely know when they've done it. It's hard to make big changes. I get it. In fact I think I can safely say I know that better than most. But it nevertheless feels like a complete negation of my very existence, almost every single time. And I fucking hate how I grant people that power over me, even for a second.

More contradictions:

A) "Of course I'm going to publish this book under my real name. I don't give a fuck who knows, and if anybody has a problem, including my kids' fucking friends' parents and our neighbors, then we don't need them in our lives anyway."

vs.

B) "Gee, I sure don't want to get strung up from that award-winning, historic maple tree at the end of the block."

And my wife's:

A) "I love and support you and your work and am 100 percent behind anything you choose to do."

vs.

B) "Do you think that the prowler who was fixing to throw a brick through our glass door but instead dropped it on the porch when the dog barked at three A.M. last night was a hate crime?"

It is far simpler to say something was broken and needed fixing. That  God made a mistake. That a boy brain was accidentally installed in a girl body. Or vice versa. Because most people understand mistakes. Even God botherers understand mistakes: love the sinner, hate the sin. Understand something mutating and just needing a little adjustment to be made right. Because anything else is too complicated. Demanding. Not black-and-white enough. Too gray. Too man-without-a-penis. Too woman-with-one. Does. Not. Compute.

My truth is, I wasn't a "man trapped in a woman's body," and I didn't "always know." What was there to know? There were no role models, not even a beaten, raped, and murdered Hilary Swank as Brandon Teena winning an Oscar to give me "hope." The only images I had were shameful, fleeting ones of sad, hulking men in ladies' clothing, bad makeup, and cheap, crooked wigs. Patchy thrift store rabbit furs tossed over linebacker shoulders. Hissed asides about "transvestites," reviled by society and not fooling anybody— even themselves.

Sure, I knew something was different about me. But every kid with half a brain and a third of a heart feels that way, and I guess I just wasn't smart or brave enough to figure it out on my own: *I know, I'll just change into a boy!* I acted like a boy (whatever that means). I acted like myself. I wore board shorts and T-shirts. Did tons of sports, climbed hillsides, played in Dumpsters, got in fights. Overall I was a pretty happy, well-adjusted kid. Outgoing, social, curious. Of course I got made fun of—the "dyke" barbs stinging the worst, for reasons I hadn't even begun to unravel. But didn't everybody's major, glaring area of vulnerability get massacred when they were kids?

Somehow, despite every external message to the contrary, I suppose I was always fairly comfortable living in my person. I never demanded to be called by a boy's name or cut off all my hair; I didn't start "developing" and then freak out and try to destroy the parts of me that didn't feel quite right. I certainly didn't like parts of my body as I grew older, wore big T-shirts and didn't celebrate any changes (except getting a drivers' license), but I didn't know that wasn't what everybody felt.

AND THAT YOU COULD DO ANYTHING ABOUT IT, ANYWAY.

Sometimes I look at my twenty-three-year-old friend Hunter, who began transitioning in early high school, and I'm like, YOU LITTLE PRICK. FUCK YOU that you get to go through life with your new name and your altered birth certificate, and nobody knows but your parents and your sister, and a few neighbors and friends of your choice, and wherever you go, you're just "the new guy"—in college, grad school, at your internships—and your parents helped you and supported you and signed fucking papers to let you see a therapist and get hormones and surgery and all these things that I didn't even know *existed* when I was your age. Mostly because they didn't actually exist; there were maybe one or two people out there who were furtively experimenting with that sort of thing. Okay, maybe a few more than that, but you couldn't just punch it up on the Internet and see thousands of photos of chest surgery results and an endless stream of meticulous blogs detailing every facet of transition, minute by minute, day by day. And there weren't big city clinics, and peers to talk to, a boundless supply of sterile syringes, and armies of people—male and female, straight, gay, whatever—who would still want to have sex with you (without paying for it). And support groups for parents whose kids think they want to change their genders.

And other times I look at Hunter and I'm like, Hey, dude. How are you doing? It's been a minute. I'm glad to have a little tranny brother, because there are things you (and a small handful of my other older buddies) understand that most people cannot. Good luck with that retreating hairline, bitch!

Kidding! I'm just jealous.

So, it took me a little more time. Sometimes I wish it hadn't. It was about information, or lack thereof. I frequently wonder whether, had I been born in the nineties instead of busy graduating high school and college, would I have chosen the path that Hunter did? When Hunter did? Would I have chosen a name like Hunter? Or Cole, or perhaps Tristan (likely the three most popular FTM names on record, by the way)? Would my folks have kicked me out of the house like so many (still) do, or would they have driven me to the LGBT health clinic in Los Angeles to get me started on my "journey" in a safe, supportive, healthy way?

I know what I would like to think, but the truth is I have no clue.

I sometimes think that I wish I had just been born male, and didn't have to become a man over my lifetime. But I probably more often think the opposite. That I am happy with where I started. Because it has made me the person I ended up. *Barf.* And I love my body just the way it is. *Barf* again. And my wife says she loves me and my body exactly how I am, which I don't believe because of something (personal) she said to me one time. Which I probably took the wrong way and totally out of context, naturally, because it was vaguely related to my biggest fear about my inadequacies and how they will one day cause her to fall out of love with me and leave me for a real man, like Harrison Ford.

The truth is, the only thing I would change about myself, the single thing I hate and consistently wish were different and never waver on—and KNOW that life would be significantly better if I could just attain... it's not that much to ask, and it may sound vain but I really don't care... I would sincerely like a measly three or four more fucking inches of height.

40 SUCCESSFUL[1] MEN OF MY STATURE
OR SHORTER

1. Woody Allen

2. Justin Bieber

3. Humphrey Bogart

4. Sonny Bono

---

1. #37 being debatably "successful," depending on your feelings about 2000's "Thong Song." I once hung around Sisqó backstage at a Backstreet Boys concert (yes, I was backstage at a Backstreet Boys concert), and I virtually towered over him, so I wanted to include him on this list because he and #40 are the only two guys I've actually stood beside in person. Though I did run into Martin Sheen, the father of #11, at a natural grocery store in Los Angeles one time, and I have to say, that dude looked about my height, too, so he could probably go on this list as well. How about that? A five-foot-five president of the United States.

5. (Lil) Bow Wow

6. Mel Brooks

7. James Cagney

8. Kenny Chesney

9. Richard Dreyfuss

10. Jermaine Dupri

11. Emilio Estevez

12. Tina Fey's husband

13. Michael J. Fox

14. Seth Green

15. Dustin Hoffman

16. Peter Jackson

17. Billy Joel

18. Charlie Kaufman

19. Nathan Lane

20. Spike Lee

21. Lil Wayne

22. Peter Lorre

23. Bruno Mars

24. Dudley Moore

25. Rick Moranis

26. Willie Nelson

27. John Oates

28. Joe Pesci

29. Roman Polanski

30. Prince

31. Daniel Radcliffe

32. Tony Robinson

33. Mickey Rooney

34. Nicolas Sarkozy

35. Martin Scorcese

36. Paul Simon

37. Sisqó

38. David Spade

39. Jon Stewart

40. Elijah Wood

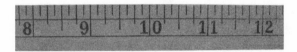

TELEPHONE CONVERSATION WITH
RE*DICK*ULOUS[1]

TC: Do you have another job besides dancing?

REDICKULOUS: I like to keep what I do personal, but yes, I have another job, at a corporate headquarters.

TC: Do your coworkers know what else you do for a living?

RD: They know, but I don't discuss it. My job knows, I talked to

---

1. Stage name of an Atlanta-based male exotic dancer who appeared on Bravo network's *The Real Housewives of Atlanta* reality TV show in late 2011. ReDICKulous is essentially known for two things: 1) his (literally) big, swinging dick, one of the largest around, and 2) his ability to perform autofellatio—oral sex with himself.

corporate, so they know.

TC: When did you start dancing?

RD: I was already a popular exotic dancer, but it really took off after the show aired. I was retiring last year, but I was requested by Phaedra [Parks, a subject on *RHOA*] to come on the show. Now I got bookings through the end of the year.

TC: But how and when did you get into dancing originally?

RD: A friend suggested I start doing it in 2007, so I entered a local amateur competition, and I won. I was the first Mr. Exotic Dancer Universe, and I've been performing internationally since two months after I started dancing.

TC: When did you realize something was different or exceptional about you?

RD: [*defensive*] I don't do that offstage, only onstage. Okay, so I know how to do it. It's like this: when I perform, that's not all I do, it's just one of my tricks.[2]

---

2. At this point, I had no idea what he was going off about… I was of course just myopically focused on his massive member as though it was the key to unlocking the secret of the universe, but then it occurred to me: he was referring to autofellatio. I had been planning to ease into the subject of autofellatio, but ever since the show, all anybody wants to talk to him about is his ability to give himself a blow job, and he was (understandably) a little chippy about it.

TC: What are some other tricks you do onstage?

RD: I don't want to give any of those away. People should come to my show to find out what I do.

TC: Oh, okay. Well, what about your other gift, the one you were born with? I mean, how did you realize you were better endowed than most guys?

RD: It wasn't something I gave any thought to. Hold on, I have another call. My momma's calling right now. [*A minute goes by*] Okay.

TC: Does your momma know what you do?

RD: Yeah, my mom and dad know.

TC: Are they supportive?

RD: Yeah, [*laughing*] both my mom and my dad are supportive of what I do.

TC: I'm, well.... Here's the thing: I'm not the most well-endowed guy. Can you tell me if there are any downsides to having a really big penis?

RD: Um, not really. Not sexually, no. But it gets annoying when everybody wants to see it, or talk about it. That's one of the downsides.

TC: Do you ever wish you were just, like, normal?

RD: Not really, no. But I am a lot of other things, too. I was in the military,[3] I went to school and got a degree. I was married, divorced. There are other things I'm known for.

TC: Like it's nobody's business unless you share it with them, or when you're working?

RD: Yeah, most people I meet don't know that's what I do outside of when they meet me. I have to invite them into that world. But if someone already knows who I am, they're a fan or something and they want to talk about ReDICKulous all the time, it never goes anywhere. In the first five to fifteen minutes, I can figure out if somebody knows.[4] So I control conversation, and I can cut it off.

TC: Are you in a relationship with anybody right now?

RD: Yes, but I know how to separate the two. I separate what I need to do when it comes to handling business and [my personal life].

TC: Has business taken off since the show, has your rate gone up?

RD: Yeah, it has.

---

3. He worked with artillery, as a cannon crew member on tanks (not making this up).

4. Dude, I get it; I have exactly the ~~same~~ opposite problem.

TC: Can you quit your regular job if you want to?

RD: Yeah, I could.

TC: What is your rate now, if you don't mind my asking?

RD: My booking fee is minimum $500, plus travel and lodging, and that's just for a walk-through appearance. If I perform, it's more like $1,000 to $1,500, plus I have a rider.

TC: What's in your rider, what do you require—

RD: Nothing sexual or anything.[5]

TC: I mean, what kind of requirements do you have for your gigs?

RD: Oh, it includes different stuff. Like a special drink for the performance, or stuff I need for the show that I can't fly with because of security hazards. But that's it.

TC: Security hazards?

RD: —

TC: What do you drink before you go onstage?

---

5. Chippy again. I swear I hadn't even been thinking anything like that.

RD: Usually 151 and Coke.

TC: What percentage of your business is gay vs. straight?

RD: I started in gay events, [but] I'd say it's half and half now. Money is money. It doesn't matter; if you book me, you book me. I don't pick and choose gay or straight,[6] I pick and choose [based] on who's about paying me and business.

TC: Do you ever just, like, not feel like it? Like, shit, I have to go do all that again, and don't feel like getting it up?

RD: When it comes to work, I know what I have to do, and I do it. And then I turn around and come back home. I don't stay in a city any longer than I have to. I mean, I've been doing this so long, I've been everywhere. I've seen all the attractions.

TC: I know a lot of guys will.... Do you ever have to supplement with Viagra?

RD: I have done it. It depends. I try not to have any sexual contact for twenty-four hours before a show, so then I don't need that.

TC: You know, there's, uh, [*uncomfortable*] so much emphasis placed on penis size in our culture, and how that does or doesn't translate

---

6. ReDICKulous identifies as bisexual, incidentally.

in the world—

RD: I'm outside right now, so I can't hear you...

TC: How big is your member, exactly? Or do you not talk about that?

RD: No, I tell people. [*quietly*] It's eleven and a half.[7] I don't like when people put that on [event] flyers, though. It kind of upsets me, because that's not anybody's business until they come to a show. You can promote my name, but never put [my penis size] on there. Nowadays everybody just puts on their flyers and radio ads that I'm from the *Atlanta Housewives* show, so...

TC: Did you hear about this guy in North Carolina who died trying to give himself a blow job?

RD: No.

TC: His heart compressed and they found him dead in bed at a weekly motel. Do you ever worry about that?

RD: No, I'm not worried about that.

TC: Well, he was apparently pretty overweight, so I guess that's probably not going to be an issue for you.

---

7. I'm 99 percent sure he means erect. FYI: The world-record largest penis is 13.5 inches (erect).

RD: —

TC: So how did you discover that you were able to do that?

RD: I was asked to do it by the MC of a show, back when I was an amateur. So I tried it, and it actually happened.

TC: Do you ever wish you were known for something else?

RD: I mean, I haven't always been known for this. People I went to high school with didn't know, but I was much smaller then.

TC: You don't remember the specific time when you realized, like, I've got more than the average guy?

RD: Well, I have a twin brother, and I'm sure he's well-endowed based on what females [he's been with] have told me.

TC: So you knew only through hearing it from them?

RD: No. There was also this one time I was sitting on the toilet, and my dick fell into the water.

TC: [*beat*] You never asked your twin brother, like, Hey, does your dick ever fall into the toilet water, or anything like that?

RD: No. I never did.

WHEN I KNEW

CENTURY 21 MAY SOUND LIKE a realtor, but if you've ever lived in New York City, you know it to be the best quality new-clothing-at-a-steep-discount-outlet in the city. Twenty-two years old, and newly a New Yorker, I found my way to the original downtown store within the first month of signing the lease on my puny six-floor walk-up tenement apartment on the Lower East Side. (This was well before it was a bridge-and-tunnel nightlife destination; on the first night I moved in, I heard gunshots in the housing development across the street. I know, I'm so *gangster*.)

Emerging from the N train onto Cortlandt Street in front of the store, I searched straightaway for the twin towers of the World Trade Center, but I couldn't find them. Not because they weren't there (like nowadays), but rather because they were directly above me, and I hadn't gazed high enough to locate where they were. Or where I was.

Pushing through Century 21's heavy front doors, I stepped into a generous, two-story atrium. I felt something pulling me past the Fendi purses and Boss belts, the Ferragamo wallets, luxurious shearling coats, toward the rear of the shop and up the first set of escalators. As I slowly ascended, seemingly ancient gears grinding beneath my soles, I could sense something twitching at the base of my neck; the tiny hairs of my recently shorn fade were standing at attention. At the top of the escalator I spotted what I'd come for: several large racks overflowing with Calvin Klein men's undergarments: T-shirts, tank tops, and...*gulp*, underwear. I glanced left. Right. Ladies streamed toward a riot of designer bras and panties, while a couple guys lazily thumbed through flat, plastic-encased packs of crew-neck T-shirts as though they were vintage LPs.

I stiffly approached a rack containing the boxer briefs, just to the left of the regular old briefs, aka banana hammocks. My cheeks burned, chest pounded, palms sweaty as I quickly sought to ascertain the lay of the land: sizes small, medium, large, and extra large; basic colors of black, white, and heather gray (or gray stripes). CALVIN KLEIN conspicuously stitched on all of the wide elastic waistbands. I reached for a two-pack of white mediums, thinking I'd keep it simple, grab and run, and recover my composure in a safer, gender-neutral section of the store. But then the guy next to me coughed, a loud, hacking TB type of number, and it seemed like he might be faking it in attempt to get everybody within earshot—including store security, the gender police—to glance in our direction. To catch me in the act of attempting to break the gender barrier.

I looked downward, trying to stay cool, at least on the exterior. Was that Marky Mark posing in black and white on the cardboard insert I now held in my hand? Demonstrating precisely what the product would look like on my body—on my *package*—should I decide to purchase it?

I want to be him filled my brain and stilled me. I grew steadier, resolute, stood a little taller. *I am him.* (Well, minus the third nipple. Or shit, I would even take the extra nipple if only I could look even a fraction like that dude.) *That's what buying these boxers will make me look like.*

The hacking cougher disappeared behind a rack, near the V-neck undershirts. Nobody seemed to be paying me any mind, and it looked as if I would be alone for a spell. I glanced back and forth between the rows of underwear and the pack I held in my hand, closely studying the product specs. I noticed something I'd missed in all my haste to vacate the men's unmentionables department—there was not one, but two varieties of boxer briefs on offer: classic boxer brief and button-fly boxer brief. Which did I want?

I made a quick decision that button-fly seemed somehow less masculine. More sensible. Less pushing my luck. Perhaps a cashier would think I was just buying them to sleep in. They're just so damn comfy!

I haphazardly stuffed the white mediums back on a rack and reached instead for two single packs of button fly boxer briefs in the same size: one striped gray, one black. Double-checked the Marky Mark look-alike for two buttons running down the fabric cradling his package, and then tucked the two items into an armpit and strode purposefully toward a carousel of Adidas workout pants. But I didn't want Adidas workout pants. Or anything else. I'd already found what I came for, and after psyching myself up for a few more minutes before choosing whichever bored clerk would launch my maiden men's undergarment voyage (excluding the requisite pairs of boxers I'd inherited from friends in high school and cherished), I waited in line between two ladies with heaps of couture in their arms and a cloud of overpowering perfume about them.

"Next? I can help you over here, ma'am."

I slid my two thin packages across the counter. The plastic crinkled loudly when the middle-aged lady scooped them up. She didn't even look at me, just scanned the items and mumbled, "Twenty-four fifty-three, cash or credit?"

I counted out two twenties. Still she didn't glance up, just pressed the change and receipt into my palm. "I don't need a bag!" I hollered, too loudly, while attempting to stuff the two pairs of underwear into my olive-drab canvas Manhattan Portage messenger bag. Then I got the hell out of there.

Once home I tore into the plastic of the gray striped boxer briefs, still breathless from the six-story climb. My little dog jumped on my leg and yapped, imploring me to take him for a walk. But he could wait. I went into the bedroom and closed the door, a shard of a mirror hanging behind it. I didn't even check whether my roommate was home; I needed to get a good, long look at myself. To see how it would feel, finally, after all these years.

I unbuttoned my jeans, one by one, trying to avert my eyes as I rolled blue cotton panties (the kind my mother still bought at outlet stores and periodically shipped to me), down my hairy legs and kicked them onto the floor under the bed. I unfurled the boxers, which were neatly folded around a rectangle of cardboard and Scotch-taped in place. I held them up and studied them for a beat before pressing them against my nose, inhaling deeply the fresh dyed cotton smell. The musk. The masculinity. Goddam Old Spice or something. Yeah!

I stepped into them.

Looked in the mirror. I still had on an Oxford-type button-down with a V-neck wool sweater over it, so I lifted both of these in the front so I could get a good look at the skivvies. Me in the skivvies. They were indeed soft, fit just right, tight enough so the trim hugged each thigh, but loose enough so that the pouch almost looked like it could have something in it. Not quite Marky Mark, but like a regular guy.

I smiled at myself. Popped a CD into the stereo and pressed play. "Boys Don't Cry" by the Cure came on. I turned it up loud, crazy cat lady neighbor across the hall be damned, and started dancing around the room. My dog nosed his way through the door then, hopped up onto the bed, and sat there staring at me. I continued to ignore him. In between fly dance moves I slid open the top drawer of my dresser and fished out some tube socks. Kneaded the wad so

it was just right… and then slipped it down the front of my boxers.
I held my thighs together a little so as not to lose my package.

I checked myself in the mirror one more time as Robert Smith
faded out and "Goodbye Horses" by Q Lazzarus began. My dog
shivered on the bed. I wondered whether he could discern the new
man I was becoming in front of him.

██

████████████████████████ The music unfurled into the
room, almost incantatory. ██████████████████████████████
██████████████████████████[1]

I pulled my sweater off over my head, quickly unbuttoned my
dress shirt, three-quarters bare-chested now. I squeezed my junk in a
fist and made a punk rock face in the mirror. Damn, I looked good. I
reached over my head and flicked the disco ball suspended from the
ceiling where a light fixture should've been. It spun and swung, re-
fracting orange late-afternoon light around the small room. I leaned
over seductively and pressed RECORD on the video camera that
was set up on a tripod beside the mirror, aimed directly at me. Then
I patted around the top of my dresser for some lipstick, popped off
the cap, and leaned in to the mirror/camera lens. I started apply-
ing the lipstick theatrically, sticking out my lips, pouting, seducing.
"Would you fuck me?" I whispered in a low growl. There was no
answer.

---

1. Song lyrics have been redacted because our request to reprint them here (for a
fee) was denied by Sony's rights office (in Tennessee). A young lady at Sony was
sent this chapter for her perusal, but upon reviewing it, she decided it was not in the
best interest of her company to allow us to include any part of the song. It was, she
said, her job to protect MGM/Sony.

"I'd fuck me," I answered myself, louder now. "I'd fuck me so hard."

I stepped back farther so the camera could get a full body view, and draped a tasseled silk tapestry around my shoulders. That's when I remembered the lady suit that I'd been sewing for months, hanging on a hook inside the closet. So I pulled out the top half of the suit and fit it over my head snugly like a wig, jagged scalp brushing my eyebrows. I slowly inched my new boxers halfway down my thighs. Got up on tippytoes and held my shawl aloft over my shoulders like some perfect, gorgeous god or something, getting a full look at my mangina in the mirror. The camera was catching all of this on tape, and the music crescendoed, and the room spun around me cinematically, and I fell back onto the bed just as the sky opened up outside my fire escape window and a clap of thunder echoed loudly through the narrow streets of the Lower East Side.

And that's the moment when I knew: I'm going to be a MAN.

I AM a man.

No, that's not what happened at all.

I just made all of that up. Well, the last bit is actually sampled from that scene in *Silence of the Lambs* when Jodie Foster is closing in on the homicidal transsexual Buffalo Bill, while his latest full-figured female victim is screaming in the dungeon below, trying to capture Bill's beloved poodle Precious with a chicken bone tied to a string. Bill dances around in the lady skin suit he is methodically fashioning by sewing parts of his victims together, forcing them to condition their skin with body lotion before he kills them.

IT PUTS THE FUCKING LOTION IN THE BASKET!

He is ecstatic, high, autoeroticizing—and clearly delusional, we are meant to gather, as he leans in to the camera and breaks female character momentarily so he can tuck his penis tightly between his thighs before striking his most feminine pose, that silky fabric draped around him as if on a cross. "Goodbye Horses" blasting,[2] the red LED light pulsing on his video camera. It's such a poignant moment because it captures precisely what all of us transsexuals do—male-to-female, female-to-male, whatever the fuck. We mutilate members of the "opposite" sex so that we can harvest their accoutrements—their skin, even—because we so despise the shell into which we were born. We weren't born in the wrong bodies; we were born in the wrong skin!

No, none of this chapter is the "truth."[3] There was never that one time *I just knew*. No seminal afternoon on which I sidled into a store to buy (or steal) my first piece of men's clothing and then sneak it home to cross-dress before a mirror to reveal my true identity in the privacy of my chamber. There was no singular, climactic, revelatory moment. No first time stepping out on the street suddenly as a man, no first time bedding a woman as a guy, no tortured decade in my

---

2. Sony/MGM was apparently fine with having their song used in this instance.

3. Well, I did—mostly in the nineties when Calvin Klein was single-handedly revolutionizing the undergarment market, convincing all men that other men and women alike would only want to fuck them if they wore Calvins—take advantage of the discounted underwear at Century 21 on a few occasions. But I soon realized that Jockey boxers were just as good, and saved my money for vital stuff, like monthly AOL dial-up fees.

twenties, loathing myself and my body, not fitting in anywhere, and unable to figure out that there was one missing piece to the puzzle that would make everything okay if I could only locate it in the shag rug beneath the coffee table.

No aha! moment. (Sorry, Oprah.)

It wasn't when I bought my first suit and tie, changed my first form of ID, corrected somebody with, "I go by 'he'" for the first time. I am finding it difficult to describe what it was. I can only seem to tell you what it was not.

Though I can say a few things with some measure of confidence: that I have always done the best I could with whatever I had—wherever I was—at any given point in my life. And that in all likeliness, I would've been able to *survive* as whatever I was had I not been fortunate enough to be in the position to pursue transition. I am, however, very happy[4] that I finally gave myself—in the third decade of life—the ability to go through the world as a man until I die.

Because it is also true that I do not particularly enjoy the image I have of myself during the years *before* I pulled on some style of boxers each morning before getting dressed.

---

4. An inadequate word for it.

DIALOGUE

THE FOLLOWING IS AN open letter to Brad Pitt and Angelina Jolie, written by Bonnie Fuller (editor of the website "Hollywood Life: Your Celebrity News, Gossip & Style BFF"). It appeared on January 4, 2010, and it is reprinted here exactly as it appears on the blog.[1]

Brangelina—what are you doing to poor Shiloh Jolie-Pitt? Your 3½-year-old daughter is getting dressed in boys clothes so often by you

---

1. Accompanying the item is a reader poll posing the question, "Do you think it's wrong to dress Shiloh like a boy all the time?" Current results: 42 percent voted "Yes! She'll be gender-confused," while 58 percent voted "No! Who cares what she wears—she's probably a tomboy."

that the New York Post *even described her today as* your *"son." And no wonder. She was photographed in daddy Brad Pitt's arms, heading in to the Broadway show,* Mary Poppins, *on Jan. 3, wearing a boy's (literally) Burton ski cap and black puffy jacket.*

In recent photos she's been decked out in a fedora, tie, camouflage pants, boy vest, pirate sword, navy knit skull and crossbones hat, black jeans, gray jackets, black and white skull socks and sneakers. Even the stuffed animal she carries is blue.

Never ever is Shiloh dolled up in anything remotely girlish. Her blond hair is hidden under hats or left unbrushed and pushed to the side of her face.

Her sister Zahara Jolie-Pitt, however, is allowed to have her girly touches. HER Mary Poppins hair was pulled into a purple barrette and a pretty bracelets [sic] escaped from under the arm of her coat.

And you're not dressing your little boys like girls!

So Brad and so Angelina—what's up with the cross-gender dressing for Shiloh? Did YOU both want another boy, not a girl? Maddox and Pax weren't enough? Aren't you worried that you're going to confuse little Shiloh? Give her gender identity issues? Isn't it hard enough to grow up without your parents dressing you like the opposite sex?

A shrink says yes.

"Angelina has said she was bisexual in public—this is her bisexuality coming through. She's saying "I'm not going to teach my daughter gender—let her pick," believes psychologist, Dr. David Eigen.

But will it confuse her? "Yes," says Dr. Eigen. "She is being guided into a bisexual role. Her mother is projecting this onto this particular child—she has chosen her as her favorite. I think this is an issue." Such an issue that Shiloh is already insisting she be called by a boy's name,

"*John.*" *Brad apparently told Oprah that Shiloh insists on being called* "*John, I'm John,*" *he explained,* "*It's a Peter Pan thing.*"

Peter Pan Thing, my ahem! Brad, does Shiloh even know what the color pink is? Has she even seen it? Why do you let little Shiloh be dressed this way?

"*All I can say is that Brad must be whipped if he allows this,*" *believes Dr. Eigen.*

Wow! Brad you're whipped! Now, come on—time to get up your gumption for the sake of your daughter and let her be a girl, if she wants to be.

—*Bonnie Fuller*

AN OPEN LETTER TO BONNIE FULLER FROM SHILOH JOLIE-PITT

Dear Mrs Fuller,

Wow, are you a stupid cunt. I am not the favoret, Zahara is, duh, and Maddox is the favoret boy. By a landslide. Everybody knows that, its an open sebret in our family. And whats this "doctor" you asked about my mom's sexual history? Is he even a doctor? I'm three and I know that what clothes somebody wears dosen't make them attracted to the same sex. that's retarded. Not to mention, I don't even know what sex is and whatever it is, I won't be having it for about 13to15 years anyway. Stop sexualizing me; its creepy, like when those ladies make their kids to strip-tease on "Toddlers and Tiaras."

Listen lady, I'm not the one who's confused; society is confused. Psyche ﹖ Gender is a socially constructed concept. Practically everything in society is assigned a gender — like toys, colors, behaviors, my Burton ski cap, and apparently even simple black jeans and a gray jackets.

My dad may be whipped, but you spend all day, every day <u>blogging</u>.

Sincerely,
John Jolie-Pitt

MY WIFE'S JOB

RIGHT THIS MINUTE MY wife is on a movie set in Louisiana, spending three straight days with Kevin Durant, one of the biggest stars in the NBA, who has been cast in a film while the league is in a lockout. She's writing a story about the guy for a leading sports magazine. Just a second ago a text popped up from my wife containing a photo of Durant sitting across a table from her at Hooters, beside a smitten female fan who'd stopped by his booth to pay homage. Later, another text pops up: him shooting some baskets solo in an otherwise empty LSU gymnasium.

You know what else my wife has done during her twenty-year career as print journalist?[1]

---

1. Since she is probably going to kill me for including this chapter, I should

She was flown over Los Angeles by Harrison Ford in his helicopter.

Rode around a racetrack with Carl Edwards in his NASCAR car, and saw him get undressed in his trailer.

Accompanied David Beckham around New York City for several days, and watched him get naked too.

Tossed footballs back and forth with Santonio Holmes, Reggie Bush (who showed her the oxygen chamber in his bedroom), Victor Cruz, and a few other players I can't remember right now.

Watched an NBA game with Jay-Z.

Talked about girl trouble with Dirk Nowitzki and Dwyane Wade.

Shopped for jeans with Liam Neeson.

Discussed books and poetry and a lot of other intellectual bullshit with Viggo Mortensen (who later sent her a bunch of expensive

---

probably add that my wife is not some twatty Hollywood celebrity reporter writing about who wore which dress better to the Oscars. She turns in smart, considered, in-depth, and always completely unique profiles of the dudes she is assigned to write about. And she is just about as low-key and discreet as it gets about being with them. Über-professional, and usually unimpressed until there's good reason to feel otherwise. (She also interviews female celebrities and athletes sometimes, though in truth she is pretty much a specialist on capturing men—*awesome*.)

What my wife does get excited for are those completely unknown and obscure, yet infinitely more interesting individuals doing incredibly cool (if sometimes more quiet) things in the world. She also writes about those things beautifully, as she can be relied upon to find the most fascinating and human moments among all sorts of people—even Ryan Seacrest—that tell us something we didn't know about the world, about ourselves. My wife is an all-around brilliant writer and poet (who also wrote an incredibly moving, not to mention award-winning, nonfiction book), an old-school bona fide journalist to whom all the clichés apply: a dying breed, the last of her kind.

artsy-fartsy books and journals that he wrote or made or collaborated on or something, which are still sitting up on our bookshelves).

Chilled with Shaun White on his bed.

Toured with *American Idol*.

Hung out on a movie set with the Rock, or whatever his original name was before he went back to being cool with "the Rock." (He sent her a couple dozen roses and chocolates after. Roses and chocolate, *really?*)

She has spent days upon days, nights upon nights, fancy dinner upon fancy dinner, with the likes of Jude Law, Matthew McConaughey, Orlando Bloom, Mark Wahlberg, Steve Martin, Nick Lachey, Simon Cowell, Ewan McGregor. I'm omitting dozens. Not to mention one in particular I'm leaving out specifically because she ended up briefly dating the douchebag (after the cover story came out).[2] I used to like the guy (or at least be neutral about him and his stupid fucking oeuvre), and now I positively despise the dude, and would gladly punch him in the cunt if given even a momentary opportunity. I change the channel immediately if his smug-ass face comes on the TV screen, glance away if he has a new movie being advertised on the sides of buses. Because I am that weak, that big of a pussy, and even though they dated for a short time something like twenty fucking years ago, I simply cannot bear the thought of that asshole FUCKING MY WIFE.

---

2. Since I'm probably already dead for including this chapter in the first place, now before my corpse is desecrated entirely, I should add that this particular guy was the only one she ever said yes to when he asked her out after their business relationship concluded.

And since I came into her life, do you know where I have been when my wife is out of town doing her job by spending time with rock stars like these? I am at home making chicken quesadillas and bag lunches and carpooling and arguing with our older child about wearing mascara to school. Checking math homework, matching Tupperware tops to bottoms, doing several rounds of back tickles before bed. Also laundry, arranging playdates with the kids' friends' annoying mothers who keep me on the phone way longer than necessary to plan one fucking sleepover. Picking up dog shit in the yard, putting up shelves in the pantry, going to the grocery—and spending any free minutes when not doing all of the above sitting in my tiny, claustrophobic office, writing my stupid little books that about twenty-seven people will ultimately read.

For her last trip before interviewing Kevin Durant, my wife was sent down to Austin, Texas where she stayed at the home of Jesse James for the better part of a week.[3] He's got giant fucking muscles, is rich as shit, still has his hair, and he forges cool stuff out of metal in a personal workshop on his compound. One day they're shooting massive amounts of ammo out of massive illegal-looking weapons together on his acres of land (and sending me videos of it). The next day she's playing with his cute pit bulls, going out to get Mexican dinner with his family, talking to his tattooer girlfriend; his daughter is hanging out in my wife's guest-house bed. The guy makes fucking whole motorcycles and cars from scratch, gorgeous fucking vintage pickups, the kind my wife has always wanted, and

---

3. There are several sides to every story.

he's just driving her around town in one of them, here, there, taking care of business—and I'm back home transferring a load of whites from the washer to the dryer, when she texts me a photo of him with a welder's mask on, making her a one-of-a-kind beer bottle opener with his signature on it (we don't even drink beer)... and I think, what the fuck can *I* do?

No, really: WHAT CAN I DO? This guy is the founder and CEO of a company that pulls in something like $200 million a year, and he makes things out of metal using his two hands... and I can daintily peck out a few words on a keyboard from time to time, and scarcely make enough cash to buy gas for the pickup he's driving my wife around Hipster Town, U.S.A., in for the better part of a week.

Most days I'm cool. I'm proud of my wife, respect what she does, and actually find it kind of amusing that she spends time with all these famous alpha dudes for a living. And that some of them have flirted relentlessly and have wanted her and had no problem making that fact known—and that she has (except that once) said no to them, that she has instead ultimately chosen ME.

But on darker days, when I am lonely and I start thinking about it too much, I don't do as well with the fact that while I am at home being SOFT, she is out there having dinners and cocktails and over-the-top adventures with men who are (generally)

Richer.

Stronger.

Taller.

Larger.

Better looking.

More culturally relevant.

More famous, thus more handsome.

More masculine.

Harder.

In my small place, my fear corner, I am certain that the latter is a problem I am powerless to thwart. A problem that might fly under the radar now, but that will eventually boil up and over when it turns out I am not enough for her. Even though she doesn't care about any of those things—I know her, I know she doesn't care—I am afraid she will someday, simply, suddenly want a real man.

And I will completely understand.

Because she has made me the man I am today. I'm not saying I wouldn't be a man if she were to kick my sorry ass to the curb; I'm just saying I would likely be a very different kind of man. A worse one.

TEN FRIENDS' FEARS[1]

1. THAT [BEING TRANS] WILL prevent me from getting love and happiness and success. It's sad being a transsexual. I feel sad about it. —R

2. Getting my ass kicked. Also I fear dying alone or being unlovable, or for people to see me as a monster in nursing home care. —K

3. That I'm going to go bald because my mother's father is. —D

4. My biggest fear is that, due to the imminent apocalypse, or socio-

---

1. I asked ten FTM friends, "What, as a transman, is your biggest fear?"

economic collapse of society, I would lose access to Vitamin T.[2] —C

5. Sexual rejection. —T

6. Cervical cancer. —G

7. Recently I've started worrying that my pee stream sounds different from cis-guys'.[3] —E

8. That my dick will fall out when I'm running on the treadmill at the gym. —L

9. Obvious stuff like yearly exams, nudity, family reunions. This year I had to face extended family as a dude at my father's funeral, though my mom still calls me her "daughter" (yes, even with a full beard), so that was awkward. —S

10. That I'm unlovable. —A

---

2. aka testosterone.

3. *Cisgender* is a respectful term for "not transgender," basically to avoid using potentially pejorative terms like "real man" and "real woman" or "biological man" and "biological woman," all of which subtly imply that transgender men and women aren't "real" or "biological" men and women.

TEN OF MY FEARS

1. THAT I MIGHT BE trading in a couple years at the end of my life so that I can live in a body more aligned with who I am now, while I am relatively young and healthy.

2. That after this book comes out, neighbors and parents at my kids' school and various other people who "didn't know" about me will find out, and then I'll be standing there choking and coughing in that burning room, with a bucketful of kerosene residue in one hand and nothing but a fist in the other.

3. That after this book comes out, I'm going to have to discuss things like feelings and thoughts and bravery and misconceptions and personal journeys toward understanding with people like my parents and other family members and in-laws and friends and shit.

4. That I am an asshole for wasting all of this time and energy writing about my stupid fucking self when maybe I should've been putting that time and energy toward something that actually matters, like building houses for people who don't have them, or getting food and water and clothing to people who don't have enough of those things either, or saving children and puppies from abuse, neglect, and skin infections. Helping occupy Wall Street, and shutting down factory farms and the Tea Party. Rescuing more pit bulls from certain death, adopting HIV-positive orphans from Malawi, volunteering to read books aloud at nursing homes, or teaching writing workshops up at the state prison. Hell, learning to play the banjo.

5. That I won't be able to support my family and myself.

6. That I will end up with a chronic health condition, go off testosterone, and then be sickly, plus stuck in some kind of purgatory.

7. That my kids will hate me when they "find out" that I've been lying to them about who I am, even if I haven't been lying—the way my brother was supposedly angry with my parents when he "found out" he was adopted, even though they'd been telling him as much since he could speak.

8. That my wife will leave me and I will end up a sad and lonely freak with nobody to truly understand and love me in my dying days, which will be spent in a run-down, woefully under-funded nursing home staffed by mean and abusive nurses who won't tend

to my bed sores because they will be disgusted (by me, not the bed sores).

9. That, like Sarah Kurtin in high school, whose only wish was not to be remembered for her perfect score on the SAT (and yet that is all I seem remember about her), I will always be known primarily for the thing I'd like not to be known for.

10. That just as quickly as I think I've managed to capture something here, it will be gone. For one, because I could wake up tomorrow and my feelings about all this (not my gender identity, just the business surrounding it) could change. And second, that even if I've managed to capture anything here, I've squandered my one opportunity to do so because I will have done merely a mediocre job of it. The impudence of trying to encapsulate any kind of a life at all, whether in the space of six hundred words—or sixty thousand.

THE SEX CHAPTER[1]

---

1. Conversation I had with my wife one recent night in bed, after sex:

    HER: Hey, are you going to write about sex in your book?

    ME: Hey, are you fucking kidding me?

    HER: That's what people always want to know about.

    ME: No fucking way.

    HER: Just asking…

    ME: Well, I'm definitely going to work in something about how I'm far and away the best sex you've ever had, ever—a world champion—but that's pretty much it.

99 PROBLEMS, AND A BITCH AIN'T ONE
Another Brief Interview with My Wife

ME: I'M THINKING OF publishing this book under the name Tyrone Cooper instead of T Cooper. Do you think it'll help at all to use a different name? Or am I deluded? Or is it *delusional?*

MY WIFE: I thought you were Tyrone Cooper. And yes. And likely both.

ME: Tell me the thing you said about art and truth again.

MY WIFE: I believe any real art is about telling the truth. That truth is the point of art. And if you aren't starting from that, if the core is something easier, less honorable, cheap, petty, small, commercial, then the art is not art at all. It may sail by, undetected. Mr.

Brainwash. But it will not resonate, won't sing like a tuning fork in the belly, won't change a fucking thing, will just be another mirror people can't resist looking in.

ME: You know how people will sometimes come up to me and say I'm "courageous"? I feel the opposite.

MY WIFE: You shouldn't. But it is still condescending.

ME: Do you remember one time when we were at the gym—last year sometime—when I was trying to decide whether or not to write this book, and I disappeared for a while and I wasn't on the track, and when I came back you asked me where I went? Well, I had been trying to locate a pen and paper to write down something I thought of while doing the incline bench press. It was this note, in fact:

IT feels kind of good to be liberated from the tyranny of the novel, almost exhilarating when that realization hits me as I stare—I can't help but stare—at the old dude across from me wearing tight, mid-thigh-length spandex, his legs spread wide and feet planted firmly on the rubber floor in between sets on the Nautilus machine that doesn't require legs to be spread in order to do the goddamn exercise. His massive, elephantine basket of sweaty flesh cradled there on the seat between his thighs, bisected perfectly by the seam running down the middle of the shorts—are those ladies' tights? I definitely have to write about things like that, what it says about gender and our culture and how he has no clue how little everybody in here wants to see his nuts and joint while they're running on the treadmill after slaving in an over-heated cubicle all day. This is so easy! A book all about me and my clever observations. No endless researching another novel—suck it, novels! Now I just have to get past the self-loathing involved in writing a memoir; the ball-crushing suspicion that the only way my shit is compelling is if I write about being a fucking freak in the world... And then it sets in, shit, I have to write about not just that guy's elephant balls, but how his elephant balls relate to ME.

So what I think I'm saying is, this isn't a memoir. It's "a mostly non-fiction book on the subject of masculinity with some biographical elements." Do you think that's going to fly?

MY WIFE: Yes. Because you are trying to say something real. And God knows we need more of that in the universe.

ME: Will you still love and respect me if I am ever accidentally referred to as a "memoirist"? I'm only doing it because, "50 told me, 'Go ahead, switch the style up, and if they hate, then let 'em hate and watch the money pile up.'"

MY WIFE: I love you when you are accidentally referred to as a woman. I think I can handle memoirist. (You really need to get over this chip about telling your story. It is the story that matters, not the form, and in a weird way, not the storyteller.)

ME: Do you sometimes wish I were a "real" man?

MY WIFE: Oh, Christ. Even you don't believe that is a "real" question.

ME: What's the worst thing that could happen because of my writing this book?

MY WIFE: Harm would come to you or our children.

ME: What's the best?

MY WIFE: *Go The Fuck To Sleep*. Not really. I don't know. The best would be that you are proud of your work, and that the work moves someone else to a better place. Maybe even you.

ME: Don't you ever get sick of having that moment of paranoia like, WHO KNOWS, AND WHAT DO THEY THINK THEY KNOW? when a new neighbor or friend or the guy fixing the roof asks what we do for a living and we answer and then the person likely sets about asking around or Googling? I'm really sick of it, so I'm going to try to stop worrying, starting… NOW.

MY WIFE: It is a necessary concern. Because the world is not as we wish it were. See: Rick Santorum. See also: *Dancing with the Stars*.

ME: How do I end the book? I probably need some sort of crescendo or sense of "resolution," but at the same time it seems like it's never really going to end.

MY WIFE: Oh, baby, this is just the beginning.

INVISIBLE

LAST CHRISTMAS MY WIFE and I took the kids to Las Vegas, where my entire family—including my parents, my brother, and all of my family from Texas—was spending a few days together for the holidays. (It's a Jewish thing.) My children had never been to Vegas, but my wife and I certainly had; it's where we eloped and tied the knot as man and wife. The first time. We did it with only Elvis as our witness (God was busy), about six months before our "official" wedding, which was at our home and attended by about 150 friends and family, most of whom did not know that we had already legally married prior to the big day. (This second wedding was "real," too, having been officiated by my childhood friend Spencer, who is a Universal Life Church minister. We had to marry earlier for legal reasons I don't need to elucidate here—it had something to do with the status of my identification documents and what the two states require.)

On this Vegas holiday with the whole family, we dive in, taking the kids for a fairly anticlimactic ride on the zip line above Fremont Street in downtown Vegas. We tour Siegfried & Roy's Secret Garden (filled with white tigers, lions, leopards—and for some reason that doesn't particularly jibe with the overall premise of the hotel— dolphins). We travel to "fake Venice" and "fake Paris" and roll through "fake New York," as our younger one deems them. We watch a volcano erupt and lava flow every hour on the hour, and dancing fountains shooting twenty-five stories up into the sky every fifteen minutes. We eat overpriced sushi. Light Hanukkah candles and open presents one night with my cousins and their kids. We eat more: crepes, Thai fusion, Brazilian, Sicilian. It is all so crazy but also somehow fitting.

But that's not all. We also take in a show. Not just any show. A magic show: David Copperfield (née Kotkin, of the Metuchen, New Jersey, Kotkins). My father, his sister, my wife and I, and our two girls get all dressed up and hop into two cabs that take us to the MGM Grand Hotel, the third largest in the world. We wind through the noisy, smoky casino and pick up our tickets. Which turn out to be great, two adjacent tables in the middle of the theater. (My mother goes out with her brother and my cousins instead; we find out later that she scored a couple thousand dollars playing craps.)

Shortly after we settle at the seats, order some popcorn and Shirley Temples for the kids, their faces glowing red in the preshow lighting, eyes giant saucers, legs kicking madly under the table in anticipation of they have no clue what is coming... a lady in all black and outfitted with an important-looking hi-tech headset approaches us.

"Good evening. How are you all doing tonight?"

"Fine, thank you," my father says, but she is not talking to him.

"I work for David," she says, now more obviously to my wife and me, "and he'd like you to be a part of the show tonight."

"Do we have to go onstage?" my wife asks. She does not like to make a spectacle of herself.

"Yes," the lady replies.

"No," my wife says directly.

And then she looks over at our kids, who are giving *Are you kidding me? Pleeeeeze?* looks.

"Well, just hear me out," the lady continues, more to me. "And you two can decide afterward whether you'd like to be a part of it or not."

I nod. She continues: "Well, we are looking for a husband and wife to come up and help demonstrate to the audience that a plate of steel that David will be passing through during the first illusion is completely solid."

The kids are speechless. Even more speechless, though, is probably my father, who is studying the lady talking to us as though we are all about to be involved in a train wreck that he is powerless to avert.

"You're married, right?" the lady asks.

"Yes, ma'am," I say, but don't add, "Right down the boulevard, in fact, by Elvis," because nobody else at the table knows that but me and my wife.

"Well, okay then," the lady says. "We'll be taking you through each step, you will always have somebody beside you, and it'll be very clear what you're to do at all times. You don't have any health problems that would preclude you from walking up stairs or going onstage?"

"Nope," I say.

"No," my wife echoes.

"Okay, then..." I say to my wife.

Her neck is flushed the way it gets sometimes. She looks so pretty.

"Okay," my wife agrees, and the lady seems pleased she has done her job, barking something into her headset. The kids are beside themselves, considering whether we'd somehow planned this all along solely for their benefit. And my father has still not spoken a word. (I don't think my aunt knew what was going on, because she was at the end of the table, and the din of the settling crowd was significant.)

About five minutes into the show, in the dark, the lady returns to collect us, leading us up and around the audience, and then down alongside the stage. There are handlers/assistants everywhere, all black-clad. David Copperfield is in the midst of a rambling joke. "Don't hold hands while you're walking up the steps," the lady reminds us, quietly. Then we are standing alone at the bottom of the stage stairs.

"I'm going to trip," my wife whispers from behind me.

"And I'm going to be laughed off the stage. Thanks for choosing to go with four-inch heels tonight," I whisper back.

"What are we doing?" my wife asks.

What we are doing is trying not to laugh, and there is a giant, at least one-and-a-half-inch-thick steel plate being suspended in the air above and in front of us, and soon David motions us onstage, and I feel an assistant's grip on my shoulder, guiding me toward the illusionist.

"Hello, sir. How do you do?" David greets me in his customary sleepy-sarcastic cadence. I shake his hand and think, *Damn, he looks good for fifty-five. Are those hair plugs?* "Your job is to examine the steel. Right this way."

And then it all becomes a bit of a blur, and I don't know where my wife has gone, cannot see her standing off to the side behind me. I look at the steel in front, the audience side, and it seems very solid indeed, and I am standing there trying to come up with a way to demonstrate to the audience that I found the plate to be solid, but soon David hands me a hammer.

"Now, hit it over and over—hard—making sure it's solid," he instructs.

I wind up, two hands on the hammer, and whack the center of the steel plate, which sounds like a gong. I whack it again, then turn to look at David. An assistant appears to relieve me of the hammer, as another brings over my wife.

"Okay, hello, ma'am, thank you for helping out," he says to her. We are both beside David, and the plate has been hoisted and spun around in the air above us. "Now I'm going to have you examine the backside."

My wife looks at the back of the plate. "You too, sir," David says to me, at which point I go over and grab my wife's ass while she is examining the steel.

"Not *her* backside!" David mugs.

Giant audience response. My wife is looking at me like, *Really, asshole? Here?* She did not know that I had, just seconds before, been directed by an assistant to grab her ass on cue (though I do admit I am guilty of doing it frequently when not onstage beside David Copperfield, too).

"You two are married, I presume?" he asks. The audience is still chuckling, and I nod yes. "So I guess he's had ample opportunity to check out the backside *before* the show."

Even more laughter.

We are escorted by assistants to step up onto the steel plate, now situated horizontally. "Make sure it's solid, really make sure it's solid," David is saying. My wife starts jumping a little. "Now, no need to do Riverdance!" The audience roars, even though it is the same bit he's been using since the Lord of the Dance single-handedly destroyed any positive memory anybody had of the nineties.

And then there are a few seconds of dead time before the assistants return, and David thanks us and prepares to lie down on a table underneath the steel plate, where he will remain until the instant he seems to *penetrate* that steel plate. He will disappear momentarily, lying there under the plate, a large sheet tossed over all of it, and then he will simply, magically reappear atop the plate. There will be lights and smoke, and the table will be spun around theatrically several times by assistants, and the music will get louder and louder. And then he will gradually start pushing up against the silk sheet, a male, human, David Copperfield–sized form slowly emerging, a nose, a head, two feet poking up, and soon the sheet will be yanked away, and there he will be on top of the plate, arms out, palms up: *ta-da!*

And there will have been no fucking way that he could've actually done it, even from up close; right there on either side of the stage, my wife and I will see *no way* that he could possibly have done what he just did. It is a trick the brain cannot figure out when presented with the evidence before it. That he was down there a few seconds ago, and he is up here now—but he did not roll to the side, nor somehow come out from underneath the plate, or go anywhere that anybody could tell in the seconds he was out of sight. *How the fuck did he do that?* every single person who is not wearing all black is wondering.

But before all that—before the illusion begins, and before it wraps up to a chorus of *whoas* and astonished applause—we are back in that sliver of dead air, and my wife is still horrified she's actually up onstage doing this, and I'm frozen and blinded by lights thinking, *What a fucking midget I must look like right now.* But in that second there is enough time for me to notice how simply lovely my wife looks in her black-and-pink dress standing beside me, her long, dark-red hair up the way I like it, the way it was at our first wedding down the boulevard, come to think of it. And I kind of made an effort that night, too: I'm in a crisp white dress shirt and a red plaid bow tie, the old-timey kind you actually have to tie yourself; sometimes you must tie and untie it several times before getting the ratio of loops to ends just right.

We hold hands in that second before stepping off the steel plate, and then there we are center stage with David Copperfield née Kotkin in Las Vegas, on full display for a full house of 750 average everyday folks including my aunt and my father, my two children. Just an average everyday married couple, nothing particularly magical or special about us at all, just what is required every night to get from one trick to the next. Practically invisible.

ART CREDITS

ACKNOWLEDGMENTS

Diane Baldwin, Cooper Lee Bombardier, Kate Bornstein, C—'s Dad, Jibz Cameron, Colle Carpenter, Maud Casey, Ian Chase, Fredrica Cooper, Steve Cooper, Sally Ellyson (and Hem), Will 95 Georgantas, Eric Gillyard, Mary Gonzalez, Peggy Hambright, Niko Hansen, Drew Jordan, Stephen Kay, Rocco Kayiatos, Téa Leoni, Evin Luehrs, Adam Mansbach, Scott McCloud, Kenny Mellman (and The Julie Ruin), Scott Miller, Rick Moody, Alex Petrowsky, Ryan Pfluger, Spencer Presler, Chris Pureka, ReDICKulous, RWSG Agency, S—'s Mom, Turner Schofield, Scott Silver, Andrew Singer, Jonnah Speidel, Darin Strauss, Johnny Temple, Dexter Ward, Geo Wyeth.

Douglas Stewart at Sterling Lord Literistic.

Vendela Vida (keenest editor—and advocate—a guy could hope for), Ethan Nosowsky, Alyson Sinclair, Brian McMullen, Adam Krefman, Chelsea Hogue, Chris Ying, and every last being at McSweeney's and *The Believer*—all class acts.

Mom and Dad Cooper.

And, my hearts: Allison, Doodle, and Till Bill.

ABOUT THE AUTHOR

T Cooper is the author of three novels, including the bestselling *The Beaufort Diaries* and *Lipshitz Six, or Two Angry Blondes*. He also edited an anthology entitled *A Fictional History of the United States With Huge Chunks Missing*. Cooper's work has appeared in *The New Yorker*, *The New York Times*, *The Believer*, and *One Story*, among others. He lives in both New York and the South with his wife, children, and two rescue pit bulls.